Oh, Didn't He Ramble

Oh, Didn't He Ramble

The Life Story of Lee Collins
as Told to Mary Collins

Edited by
Frank J. Gillis *and* John W. Miner

with Forewords by
Danny Barker *and* Art Hodes
and an Afterword by
Max Jones

UNIVERSITY OF ILLINOIS PRESS
Urbana and Chicago

Illini Books edition, 1989

© 1974, Afterword © 1989 by the Board of Trustees of the University of Illinois
Manufactured in the United States of America
P 5 4 3 2 1

Library of Congress Cataloging-in-Publication Data

Collins, Lee, 1901–1960
   Oh, didn't he ramble : the life story of Lee Collins / as told to
Mary Collins : edited by Frank J. Gillis and John W. Miner ; with
Forewords by Danny Barker and Art Hodes and an afterword by Max
Jones.
     p. cm. — (Music in American life)
   Discography: p.
   Bibliography: p.
   Includes index.
   ISBN 0-252-06081-4 (alk. paper)
   1. Collins, Lee, 1901–1960. 2. Musicians—United States—
Biography. I. Collins, Mary Spriggs. II. Gillis, Frank.
III. Miner, John W. IV. Title. V. Series.
[ML419.C64A3 1989]
788.9'2165'092—dc20
[B]
                                           89-4871
                                             CIP
                                             MN

Contents

Oh! Didn't he ramble, ramble,
He rambled all around, in and out of town,
Oh! Didn't he ramble, ramble,
He rambled till the butchers cut him down.

— James Weldon Johnson and
Bob Cole (© 1902), from
traditional sources.

Preface

Lee Collins began telling his story in 1943. From that time, he began writing and dictating to Mary Spriggs, later to become his wife, details of people, places, and events that had been a part of his life in New Orleans, Chicago, and elsewhere.

The story began to take shape in the ensuing years, and in 1959 John W. Miner began editing the preliminary draft of the manuscript which had been prepared by Lee and Mary Collins in longhand and typescript. The raw material was arranged in chronological sequence, gaps were filled in through exchanges of correspondence with Mary Collins, punctuation was standardized, and spelling was corrected to conform with generally accepted spellings of place and personal names with which Lee had had contact. Early in 1960 Lee's illness became critical, and it was impossible for Miner to obtain further information. It was unfortunate that the editing of the manuscript was not begun years earlier.

After Lee's death on July 3, 1960, the manuscript lay fallow for a number of years, with an occasional attempt by Mary Collins and others to find a publisher. A small portion of the original manuscript was published in the *Evergreen Review* for March, 1965, with an introduction by Martin Williams.

Editorial work leading to the present publication was begun in 1972. No major alterations were made in the earlier manuscript, the only modifications being the adjustment of the chronology at certain points, the addition of information provided by Lee himself through phonorecorded interviews held with Richard A. Waterman (1951) and Bill Russell (1958), and additional corrections in the spelling of place and personal names. Lee's story was further expanded through the addition of prefatory matter, photographs, an epilogue, a discography, a bibliography, and an index.

A number of individuals were helpful in the preparation of the finished work. I am especially grateful to Bill Russell, who checked and corrected the New Orleans chapters and supplied photographs and information, and to John Steiner, who made corrections and comments on the Chicago chapters and contributed phonorecordings. I am deeply appreciative to others who made major contributions: Danny Barker wrote of his early experiences with Lee and provided photographs; Richard Allen made available copies of materials held by the New Orleans Jazz Archives and offered information on illustrative materials and phonorecordings; James D. Gordon and William Page loaned their collections of photographs and phonorecordings of sessions in which Lee participated. Valuable bibliographic and discographic data were received from Walter C. Allen, Roy Burchell (*Melody Maker*), Charles Delaunay (*Le Jazz Hot*), Janice B. Lewis (*Chicago Daily News*), Warren F. Nardelle, Sr. (*New Orleans Times-Picayune*), and Clive Wilson (New Orleans Record Company).

I am also thankful for permission to use photographs from the collections of Paul "Doc" Evans, Ralph Jungheim, John Kuhlman, Len Kunstadt (*Record Research*), Joe Mares, and Jacques Wolfsohn. Others who were kind enough to provide information were Martha Bendich of the New Orleans Jazz Museum, Enos "Doc" Cenardo, Frank Driggs, Sherwin B. French, Larry Gara, Jimmy Granato, Johnny Lane, Mary Frances Miller, Hugues Panassié, William Price, Barbara Reid, James D. Schacter, Duncan P. Schiedt, and Victoria Spivey.

My sincere thanks, as well, go to the musicians who performed with Lee Collins on the recording which is a part of this book — Pud Brown, Don Ewell, Burt Johnson, Dale Jones, Scotty McGlory,

Preface

Smokey Stover, Ralph Sutton, Booker T. Washington, and George Winn — and for the permission for use here by those musicians who are still living, and by the American Federation of Musicians and Radio Station KCBS, San Francisco.

I would like to acknowledge here my two chief sources for the spelling of place and personal names: *New Orleans Jazz: A Family Album,* by Al Rose and Edmond Souchon (Baton Rouge: Louisiana State University Press, 1967); "Thirty Years of Chicago Jazz," by Paul Eduard Miller, and "Chicago Jazz History," by Paul Eduard Miller and George Hoefer, both in *Esquire's 1946 Jazz Book* (New York: A. S. Barnes & Co., 1946), pp. 1-13, 14-38.

Finally, I am grateful for editorial assistance given by my wife, Ruth, and by Diane Chapman, who also typed the final manuscript and assisted in the preparation of the index.

Frank J. Gillis

xi

Foreword

In the frantic jazz decades 1910–30 New Orleans boasted a multitude of great players who engaged in battles of music in street parades — at balls and picnics — on trucks, on wagons — in honkytonks — just about any place music was played. During those years these battles of music were many times promoted as such, with placards and posters on street-corner posts advertising the events.

There was the challenge on the spot before a crowd or audience; there was the attitude — the general pattern of battling on your instrument for prestige, honor, superiority — "I'm Boss," "I'm King," "I'm the Greatest." And when you met a rival on your instrument — especially if you were a cornet player — a battle was expected by the crowd, fans, music lovers. So you blew, and somebody was blown away — blown out — and the news spread rapidly of the happening — in detail. And in the jazz discussion, the argument, somebody could always tell of being on the scene at jazz battles that were the talk of New Orleans — the legendary battles of

> King Oliver vs. Freddie Keppard
> Bunk Johnson vs. Manuel Perez
> Louis Armstrong vs. Buddy Petit
> Joe Johnson vs. Bunk Johnson
> Kid Rena vs. Buddy Petit

> Sam Morgan vs. Chris Kelly
> Louis Dumaine vs. Tig Chambers
> Red Allen vs. Kid Thomas
> Kid Punch Miller vs. Buddy Petit
> Lee Collins vs. Kid Rena
> Lee Collins vs. Chris Kelly
> Lee Collins vs. Sam Morgan

In the twenties in New Orleans the name of Lee Collins was often heard among the jazz lovers who argued pro and con as to who was the greatest cornet player in town, for Lee Collins engaged in many jazz battles and most times was the winner.

I joined the Jones-Collins band in 1928, and for me, a youngster in New Orleans, that meant I was a professional in the big time — let's say, like baseball — out of the minor leagues, into the majors. Lee Collins liked me and treated me like a little brother — constantly advising, counseling, tutoring me about all the things in being a jazz musician — right, wrong — good, bad — what to avoid. Lee helped many youngsters — black and white, orientals. If you loved jazz, Lee loved you. He was a New Orleans jazz man through and through. He was interested in nothing but jazz music — nothing else in the way of work interested him . . . jazz . . . jazz . . .

Danny Barker

Lee Collins? Sure, he's easy to remember. Like there's guys you miss. You know, it gets lonesome. You look around an' they're gone. Irreplaceable guys — carried their own weight. And almost all of these greats (with very few exceptions) were very quiet about their greatness. They stood tall. That's the way I remember Lee Collins.

When did we meet? I can't date it — late 40's. It was Chicago, and I'd brought Ed Hall with me from New York to do a one-nighter. It was a good band — enjoyable. But Lee and I didn't really get together 'til 1950, when I brought (the late) Pee Wee Russell, clarinet; Chippie Hill (also gone on), vocals; and Fred Moore, drums. The Blue Note (and that club is gone, too) had beckoned, and I responded. It was to be an all-star jazz band. We were joined by Floyd O'Brien, trombone (yeah, he's passed on) and Lee Collins. Hey, you remember the quip, "I never knew what happiness was 'til I got married"? Well, that's the way it was the first four weeks we were there. It was so fine. Lee, Floyd, and Pee Wee made a moving front line. No problems. Collins was a lead man; he fussed with the melody, and that gave the players on each side of him room to do their individual jobs without worrying about a trumpet player who was roaming their territory. Musically (and as far as I knew, every other way) Lee Collins had been reared right.

But one day, management informed me of the great plan. "You see, Art, we're goin' to build the ALL-Stars. And you can stay here as long as it takes to build this band up. Then we hit the road behind Louie [Armstrong]. So we plan to have Sidney Bechet [who could argue against that?], Wild Bill Davison, and Georg Brunis, and we'll get you Zutty Singleton." So, almost immediately Moore and O'Brien left, and within a couple of days the s—— hit the fan.

All through the band eruptions that followed, Lee kept his cool and played his horn. We never got any further along the all-star trail. Within eleven weeks, a job that could have endured six months went that-a-way.

Lee? He found places to play around town. And we would meet at John Schenck's Sunday afternoon sessions. How well I remember Collins standing next to Dizzy Gillespie at a Dixieland session, doing his thing. Diz heard we were throwing a benefit for a brother musician, and he dropped in to blow and offer his services. The same kind of thing Lee would do. You know, there's not much you can say about a guy who does his job well and doesn't screw up in any way. You just remember nice scenes. Like when I first hired a young chap, a horn man, Muggsy Dawson. And I liked the direction he was taking musically. So I dug into his background, and I find out that Muggs was hanging around Lee Collins. He was sittin' an' lis-tenin'. And then Lee would invite him up on stage and get him to blow alongside of Lee. And that's how Dawson was becoming a jazz trumpet man.

Collins, like many another great jazz player, just didn't take up enough "earth" time. Been here an' gone. But he lit a match, and he made a powerful noise. Those of us who heard him, remember . . .

ART HODES

Oh, Didn't He Ramble

1

New Orleans — the Early Years

My grandfather John Collins was a native of the West Indies. During the course of his life he worked as a seaman, lodge builder, and cornet player. He was an ambitious young man, and though he loved to play music he had to do other work to make a decent living.

There wasn't too much money to be made on the islands, so he took to the sea. While on one of his trips to England, he met Laura Leeds, who became my grandmother. It must have been "love at first sight," as they were married within a short time. My grandfather saved his money and brought his bride to the United States to live. They settled down in New Orleans, Louisiana, where they had six children — four girls and two boys. The daughters were Evangeline, Nettie, Ada, and Laura, and the sons were Oscar and John, Jr. John Collins, Jr., was my father.

As I said, my grandfather was an ambitious, smart man. Besides playing music, he had a shoe store on Decatur Street. He also went all over the countryside around New Orleans putting up lodge houses. The last bands that he played with were those of Lorenzo Tio, Sr., the great clarinetist, and Charlie Blaze. Lorenzo Tio, Sr., came from Mexico to New Orleans and married a Creole girl there. How well do I remember Mr. Tio and his long goatee. He was a great friend of the family and he used to carry me around on his shoulders.

My grandfather was determined that his children should get a good education, so all but one of them went to Southern University in New Orleans. My Uncle Oscar was the only one that was not forced to go to the university. In fact, he was not forced to do much of anything at all and was very spoiled. One thing that Uncle Oscar did like to do, though, was play on his trombone. He did that very well.

My father, like my grandfather, was also a cornet player and a seaman. He got the "salt water fever" and ran away from home and joined the navy, where he was made a bugler boy. He got so good on the bugle that all the other sailors would say he sounded just like he was playing a cornet. One day while President Theodore Roosevelt was aboard the ship, the commanding officer had my father to play for the president. President Roosevelt gave him a fine compliment on the sounds that he made from his bugle. Of course, this was a great honor for my father, and he has talked about it all his life.

While my father was still in the navy he met my mother, Stella Whavers. After promising her that he would settle down and stay home, they got married. But it wasn't long before he got the wanderlust and broke his promise. He joined Billiken Sam's band and went away on a tour of Europe. In England they did a command performance for the king and queen. After the tour was over my father came back to New Orleans to settle down again and went to work playing in Lorenzo Tio's band.

I came into the world on October 17, 1901, in a house at Delachaise Street and Robertson — my mother was also born in the same house. It was in the Uptown section known as the Garden District. My grandmother Laura named me Leeds after her surname. My grandmother used to tell me that grandfather was so crazy about me that he made me a pair of boots, which was my first shoes. Every stitch was perfect. After me came my brother John, then Clarence, and then Thaddeus, who I call Teddy.

Due to the extreme heat in New Orleans, my grandfather went across the lake and bought up a lot of land around Gulfport, a fast, upcoming town then. It was on the coast right on the Gulf of Mexico, so many people had summer residences there. Also, there were a lot of sporting people in Gulfport in those days. My grandfather gave each of his children a home there. He ran a saloon and restaurant at the Gulfport railroad station, which did a lot of business catering to white customers.

The worst thing that ever happened to me was in March, 1908, when my mother died. That left my father with four little boys to take care of. I was six years old and Teddy was only ten months.

The last I remember about my mother was on the day that she died. She drank some milk that was left out on the back porch. I'll never forget how pretty soon after that she started to groan and ran to me, pulling at me and telling me to go get my father. Then she lay down on the bed with my brother Teddy in her arms. My father was such a funny sort of man that the neighbors were all afraid to come over to see about mother, so I ran all the way to where he was working. I told him to hurry home, something was wrong with mama, that she was crying and could not get up. So my father ran back to the house, with me trotting along behind him as fast as the legs of a six-year-old could go. But mother was already dead when we got there. My little brother was trying to nurse from her; that was a sight that will never leave my mind as long as I live.

Before my mother died she once had made my father promise that if he outlived her he would never let any of us boys play music. She believed music was the world's worst way to make a living! But, sad to say, I had music in my soul.

Now, my father was not a jazz (it was called "ragtime" in those days) cornet player. He played legitimate, minstrel shows and such, and if he had stuck to it he would have been the pride of New Orleans. But he always did like to do sideline work.

I took to slipping father's cornet out of its case and practicing while he was at work. Pretty soon I got so that I could play some of the tunes I heard him play. My favorite was one called "At the Animals' Ball." One evening when I was practicing I heard my father coming home, so I put his cornet back in the case fast — only upside down. He was going to play that night, so it was my bad luck that he opened the case and found that the instrument was in it the wrong way. He began cursing up a storm and wanted to know who had been fooling around with his cornet. I broke down and cried; then I told him I had been practicing on the sly and could play some tunes. He reminded me that my mother hadn't wanted any of us kids to play music, but that didn't discourage me; I would just sneak off somewheres and practice anyway.

As it turned out, all of my brothers also played cornet. John, who we called Buddy, stuck to it longer than Clarence and Teddy did, though. Buddy played for a long time with a band in Pittsburgh but finally got tired of the music business and went back to Gulfport, where he settled down with a wife and became a plaster contractor. Clarence was a pretty good cornet player, too, but like our father and grandfather he ran off to sea when he was only thirteen years old. He later became the chief steward on his ship. My other brother, Teddy, took more after our mother's side and looks just like her brother, our Uncle Walton. He didn't keep up with music like the rest of us.

I mentioned the fact that after my mother passed away my father was left with four little boys to take care of. He had such a hard time raising us that my brothers and I got separated later. Aunt Evangeline, my father's sister, took Clarence, and I went to live with my Aunt Mabel, who was a sister of my mother. (Mother also had four other sisters, named Birdie, Miriam, Gertrude, and Esther, and four brothers, who were Charlie, Ralph, Floyd and Walton.) After I had gone to live on Louisiana Avenue with Aunt Mabel and her husband, who I always called Uncle Ernest, I began to get over the grief caused by my mother's death. I found some new friends; one in particular was a boy by the name of Curtiss Scott. I kept on studying my music, too, and really fell in love with my cornet. It was just a beat-up old horn my father had discarded, but it served my purpose.

My grandmother enrolled me in school,[1] which was all right itself, but I had a mean teacher, and she almost made me hate it. Uncle Ernest would pass by the school every day to make sure I was there. I was a very apt pupil and could learn fast. In the meantime, my father got married again because he was not able to take care of my two other brothers, what with Teddy being so small. But as things turned out, my stepmother was not the kind of mother that my father wanted her to be.

---

[1] In his phonorecorded interview with Bill Russell (June 2, 1958) Lee mentioned the Thomy Lafon School.

6

While I was visiting my father one summer it happened that my stepmother's niece and nephew were visiting her at the same time. When it came mealtime she would always give them their food first, and my brothers and I got whatever was left. I don't know what she thought we were, but she fed us like we were some kind of animals. And she gave her niece and nephew my mother's good plates to eat from; the "straw that broke the camel's back" was when she let that niece of hers use the special plate that I always used. So my brothers and I had to eat off tin plates and drink out of tin cups. The fight was on, but of course she won out.

One day I found a nickel, so I bought a loaf of bread at a bakery, not liking my stepmother's biscuits. As soon as I got home with the bread she took it away from me and gave all the other children some. By the time she got around to me there was nothing left but the heel. I went outside and cried. Another time, my little brother Teddy was out playing in the yard and found my stepmother's rat (a kind of hairpiece). He took it in the house to give it to her, but the rat had got full of sand, so she struck him and accused him of taking it outdoors in the first place. But it really was her niece that did it. I felt pretty bad about my stepmother hitting Teddy, and I wanted to go back home to Aunt Mabel and Uncle Ernest. They never so much as scolded me, let alone ever hurt me.

One day after I went back home to my aunt's house I happened to meet Fred "Tubby" Hall, older brother of Minor Hall. Tubby asked me how I'd like an after-school job working for a doctor. I told Tubby I would like that fine, so I went to work for Dr. Greau for two and a half dollars a week.

I remember my aunt used to wash Dr. Greau's silk shirts for him. One day I put on one of the doctor's shirts, got out my Uncle Ernest's Stetson hat that I loved to wear, and jammed his .38 Colt revolver into the waistband of my trousers. Then I went back of Alkus's box factory to do a little gambling with the boys when they got off from work. I no sooner got there than the police squad rolled up and grabbed me. It was a lucky thing that they didn't search me right away and find my uncle's gun on me. I threw it away the first chance I got.

I was taken to the Twelfth Precinct. In court that night I was fined twenty-five dollars or thirty days in jail. I hadn't done anything, but they called it loitering. There would always be some shyster hanging around New Orleans night court to get you out on bail, pay your fine, or represent you in court, whichever it happened to be. You could pay the lawyer so much a week — and don't think for a minute that he would not be around for his money every week.

Well, of course, Uncle Ernest missed his gun and raised holy Cain about it. He asked my Uncle Walton if he had it, but Uncle Walton said no, he hadn't seen it. Uncle Walton was sitting in a chair, and Uncle Ernest asked him once more if he took that revolver, and at the same time he fired away with another gun, blowing a big hole in the back of the chair. I wanted to confess right then and there that it was me that took the revolver, but I was scared to death and ran out of the house, thinking that Uncle Walton was dead — which he wasn't. Later I did tell Uncle Ernest the truth, and he only said that I should have told him before. He said that he hadn't intended to kill Walton, only scare him, as it was true that Walton did take things away from the house.

My Uncle Ernest was what they called in New Orleans a "humbug" fellow — one that was always looking for trouble and always ready to shoot at the drop of a hat. He went along with all the other toughs that were in the city at that time; he was rough on everybody except my Aunt Mabel and me. None of the dealers or players in the cotch rooms ever wanted him around. If Uncle Ernest couldn't get any chips at the gambling tables, he would sit down and call bets anyway, even if he had no money. When he lost or the banker wouldn't pay off, he'd just as soon pull out his gun and hit somebody over the head or cause some other trouble. When Uncle Ernest did something real serious, the police would come by the house and leave word for him to report to the Twelfth Precinct.

Now, a lot of New Orleans people believed in "hoodoo," so on Friday night Uncle Ernest would stay up late and sew a lot of little bags that he made out of red flannel. He sold these as "magic" to the country folks that came to town Saturday nights.

Our standard Sunday dinner was chicken, gumbo, potato salad, or some kind of roast. For dessert we had bread pudding because I liked it so much. I remember one time that Uncle Ernest's luck at selling the red flannel bags wasn't so good, so there was no money for dinner this particular Sunday. He went out in the yard and

8

killed some pigeons and set about to cook them for our dinner. But those pigeons didn't act like they would ever get done.

I got hungrier and hungrier, and Uncle Ernest kept on saying, "In a little while, son, in a little while," but I don't believe the pigeons ever did get cooked. Anyway, I finally left and went to the Chinaman's, at Tulane and Rampart Streets, where you could get red beans and rice for a nickel a bowl and chicken dinners on Sundays for fifteen cents. I only had one nickel, so I ordered a bowl of red beans and rice for dinner. A lot of kids were ashamed to let anybody know that they ate only red beans and rice for Sunday dinner because it was considered a dish for the poorer families.

My Aunt Mabel never did do much drinking, but when she had company at home she would take a glass of beer or two with them. In those days women wouldn't go into saloons, so my aunt used to give me a dime and send me out for a bucket of beer. Instead of buying a dime's worth, though, I asked for only a nickel's worth. I'd drink all I wanted, then shake the bucket up, bringing the foam bubbling up on top to make it look as if that old bucket was still full. I didn't believe my aunt caught on to this trick I was pulling, for she'd only smile and say, "This bucket sure did go fast, son. You'll have to run out and get me another one." Finally, though, she outwitted me — she greased the inside of the bucket with butter so that it wouldn't foam up!

My aunt was a real pig for jelly cake. One day she made one, and to make sure I would get enough for myself I paid her a dollar. The fact was, she had made two jelly cakes, but I didn't know that until later, so I ate mine without giving anyone else a piece. Then my aunt brought in the second one, and right away I wanted some of that, too. She cured me of being greedy then and there, once and for all! My aunt and uncle ate all their jelly cake and wouldn't give me a bit of it. I couldn't hardly believe what was happening. Now, I always had plenty of food to eat, so I guess my aunt figured it was high time to teach me a lesson. It worked, because from that day to this I never hogged any food.

We had a young girl named Juanita who stayed at our house when we were living out at 2319 Louisiana Avenue. She used to call me her boyfriend, meaning it as a joke, but I didn't take it as one — I was a pretty big boy by then, and I believed her. One day this girl and her real boyfriend got into an argument, and he slapped her, so when I saw that I ran up to him and knocked him down. He was afraid to hit me back on account of Uncle Ernest. My Aunt Mabel was some shocked, and she told Juanita not to play with me that way — that she would get me into trouble or the other way around.

I still liked to gamble, even after that time I got hauled away to the Twelfth Precinct. Once, Curtiss Scott and I were playing "pitpat," and a gang of boys were watching us. Curtiss said I was cheating, and of course that made me mad, so I threw the kerosene lamp at him, almost setting him on fire. We just about wrecked my aunt's house. When my Uncle Ernest got home and found the house all torn up like that he naturally wanted to know what had happened. After I told him, he set to work trying to put everything back in order. But the only thing he said to me was, "Son, we better get this house straight before your aunt gets home."

I used to get a big kick out of watching the peddlers on Sunday mornings. They would holler, "I got shrimp, lady! Nice fresh shrimp, lady, right out of the lake; shrimp, lady!" Now, most of them did not have licenses, so as soon as they spotted the police they would start whipping up their horses and away they'd go down the street with their wagons swaying from side to side. Sometimes they got caught.

Walking down Rampart Street one day, I spied a cornet for sale in a pawnshop window. I went in, and the man told me that the price of it was eighteen dollars, so I paid fifty cents down and fifty cents every week from the money I made working for Dr. Greau until I finally got that horn out of the store. I was only thirteen years old at that time. It was my first horn, a fat little cornet called a J. W. Pepper, made in Philadelphia. I commenced practicing and practicing. First my father wanted me to be a legitimate musician and read a lot of music, but I didn't like that. I wanted to be a real ragtime musician. I'd heard so much about Buddy Bolden since I was a kid. I didn't get a chance to see Buddy because I was a little too young when Buddy took sick, so I commenced listening to Bunk Johnson, who was in the Eagle Band.

Meantime, I got to know a blues piano player, a boy named

Preacher Dixon. Preacher took me with him to house parties and other places where he was working, and I would play along with him on my cornet. I got to the point where I could drive down some pretty mean old blues.

The gang that I ran around with in those days was Curtiss Scott, who I mentioned before, Thomas Williams, Herbert Brown, Levi Rounds, and Funny Davis. Funny stayed back at the Waifs' Home run by Captain Jones, where Louis Armstrong went as a boy, more than he did at his own place. Levi Rounds never did do any work. He got the nickname of "Stack o' Dollars," I remember, because he used to get his money changed into one-dollar bills and stack them up on top of each other to make it look like he had a whole bundle of money.

One day this bunch decided to put on a minstrel show. Three girls, Gertrude Sparks, Shakum Babe, and Rosa Brown, got some gunny sacks and sewed them together for a tent. Levi Rounds fixed up a guitar out of a cigar box, Curtiss Scott made a bass drum from an old washtub, Thomas Williams used a box and some ropes for a bass fiddle, and of course I had my cornet. We practiced evenings and put up our tent on Louisiana Avenue where the Flint-Goodridge Hospital is now. We decided to let Funny Davis sell tickets, and we set the admission price at one cent for girls and two cents for boys.

Finally, the big day came for our minstrel show. The girls danced to the tune of "Ballin' the Jack," which was popular then. We drew a big crowd and just knew that we had earned maybe fifteen cents apiece. But then someone asked for Funny Davis — and lo and behold, he had run off with all our profits!

It seems like there have always been teen-age gangs. New Orleans was no different that way than any other city. The Uptown boys wouldn't allow the Downtown boys in their territory, and in the same way, the Uptown bunch could not go Downtown without running into a mess of trouble. The Uptown bunch from the Garden District, I recall, was Baby Young, John Samuels, Brother Tillman, Skeeter, Tom McGhee, Cream-Eye James, Funny Davis, Black Gold, Hardy Givins, Oscar Dimes, and a boy from Jones's Home that was called Number Eleven. Although Curtiss Scott and me were from Uptown, too, we didn't consider ourselves members of this gang and didn't run around with them. All the same, we knew what to expect if we left from up there and went Downtown.

The Creole boys from Downtown were Steel-Arm Johnny, Dirty Dog, Yellow Yam, Teascha, Frenchy, Gray Eye, Low Shoto, and Bud Eye.

One day I went with Curtiss Scott down to the Fair Grounds when the Onward Brass Band and the Eagle Band were playing there. We found some of the other Uptown boys were there, too, so trouble started with the Downtown gang. Now, as it happened, the Downtown bunch always thought that I was a Downtown boy. So the first thing, Bud Eye waved at me and yelled, "Hi, Lee," wanting me to join that gang in the fight. The Downtown boys tore into the fellows from the Garden District and sent them flying back Uptown. As for me, I just stayed down there at the Fair Grounds, listened to the music awhile, and then went on home.

I got paid back good later on for not helping the Uptown boys, but in an odd way. One evening Funny Davis and me took a notion for some oyster loafs, so we went to Third and Franklin Streets where there was a gin joint run by Frank Fabulo, an Italian. I left Funny outside while I went in to get the loafs. The boys from the Garden District were waiting for me when I came out. Remembering the beating they had taken from the Downtown guys, when I hadn't helped them any, they knocked me down. Funny tried to tell them that I was from Uptown too, but it was too late; I had a big hickey on my head. I was never bothered any more after that, though.

Mardi Gras was always a bad time for those that had enemies. The tough guys were the Creole Wild West, the Yellow Pocahontas, the Wild Men, and the Tchoupitoulas. The Wild Men, in fact, were so bad that the police finally made them quit masking. The Indians, as they were called, would send out spies, and then the gangs tried to find each other's spies; there would be eerie yells when they did. Also, they all performed their own war dances. That was something to see! The battles between the Indians were not sham battles; they used real hatchets and real spears. The Seminoles even rode horses bareback up and down the streets. The Seminoles were Cream-Eye James, Brother Tillman, and that gang. Gertrude Sparks was the spy for them. All of the Indians had their "queens." Each "tribe" made their own costumes. They cost hundreds of dollars, and it took months of work to sew on beads and color the feathers, each gang trying to outdo the others in workmanship. As soon as one Mardi Gras was over they'd start right away getting ready for the next year.

Some of the clubs that turned out for Mardi Gras were the Zulus, the Money Wasters, the Merry-Go-Rounds, the Young Men's Olympians, the Jolly Boys and the Jolly Girls, the Longshoremen, the Pelicans, and the Baby Dolls.

"King of the second line" was One-Leg Horace. And there was Shakum Babe and Tute Ma, a great big fat woman that weighed about three hundred pounds.

The Mardi Gras season was a very busy time for musicians; they either had to make money then or else leave the city to find other jobs after Mardi Gras was over. New Orleans was a strict Catholic city, so there was very little work to be had by musicians once Lent started. But as Mardi Gras time was near, all the great musicians would sign up for jobs.

The carriage drivers' parade was another great affair every year. The carriage drivers would have on frock-tail coats and tall beaver hats, and at night they had lanterns all lit up. The carriage drivers hired the Onward Brass Band, Tig Chambers, and, in fact, all the great brass bands to play for these parades. The musicians would include Joe Oliver, Bunk Johnson, Tig, Buddy Petit, Sidney Bechet, and lots more.

All the kids followed those parades as far as we could go. New Orleans did not have many paved streets then, so it was easy to get stuck in the mud if you weren't careful. In the summer, when it was hot and dry and sultry, the dust whipped into your face and you could smell the dead in the cemetery. At night the big New Orleans mosquitoes sang "cousin" around your ears until they found a nice place to get plenty of blood for their dinner.

Walking through the streets at night you would often come across houses that had red lanterns hanging outside to let people know that a fish fry was going on inside. If you came back the same way again later on, you'd see the Black Maria pulling away, filled up.

I remember one particular day when I was following a parade that Joe Oliver was the head of. The custom then was that the boys would carry the musicians' instruments when they weren't being played on. This was considered quite an honor, so I tapped Joe on the shoulder and asked to carry his cornet. He gave it to me, and after a while I slipped the horn out of its case and started playing. Joe watched me for a time, then he turned around to the other musicians and said, "Just look at that little s.o.b. blow." Joe always cursed like that when he talked.

I kept on learning all I could on my cornet. I went to "Professor" Jim Humphrey to take lessons so I could learn to read music. I already knew my scales, of course, but you also had to be able to read in order to be a good musician.

It was about this time that Aunt Mabel left Uncle Ernest. In a way, that was the cause of me getting closer to the Eagle Band. Uncle Ernest never acted like he was jealous of my aunt, but one day when she got home he asked her for some reason or other to take him to the place where she worked. That made Aunt Mabel mad, so she got his gun out of the armoire and took a shot at him. You should have seen Uncle Ernest tear out; it was too hot for him at home! After that, Aunt Mabel was afraid to stay there any more, so she told me she was leaving but that I better stay with Uncle Ernest because I loved him so much. But I cried and said that I wanted to go with her. Tough as he was, though, Uncle Ernest was always very kind to me. Never once did he scold me or say an unkind thing to me, so that to this day I have the love for him just like he had been my own father.

Anyway, Aunt Mabel and I left home and moved Downtown on Gasquet Street, only two blocks away from Funky Butt Hall where Buddy Bolden used to play in his heyday. Gasquet, which had many big Negro cabarets, was a short street that ran from South Liberty to South Claiborne. A lot of underworld characters lived or hung out on Gasquet.

Now, Bunk Johnson had his Eagle Band at Funky Butt Hall when Aunt Mabel and I came into that neighborhood. In this band was a trombone player — and a great one, too — by the name of Frankie Duson. The musicians all said that I looked like him.

Sidney Bechet, a young clarinet player, was also in the Eagle Band at this time. When I came into the place the musicians hollered at Frankie, saying, "Hey, Duson, look — here comes your little boy." Sometimes I would pick up Bunk's cornet and play some of the tunes that I heard him play; one of them was "All the Whores Like the Way I Jazz." Bunk would go out on the sidewalk (the banquette, they call it in New Orleans) and blow his horn, and pretty soon the place would be full of people. Of course, no one went to Funky Butt Hall but roustabouts, pimps, whores, and such.

They had a bouncer by the name of Foots. That wasn't his real name, of course, but he had such big feet that the nickname Foots came to be tagged onto him. Foots would let me come in and sit on the bandstand right alongside Bunk. It used to get pretty rough in there sometimes, and then Foots would tell me, "Lee, you got to go home now." So I would leave and go home to practice on my cornet some more. Aunt Mabel told me, "You will wake up the neighbors' son, Lee." But I didn't care about that because no one ever slept much in that neighborhood anyway.

One day I happened to run into Uncle Ernest. He was glad to see me and asked me, "Son, take me to where you and your aunt live." So I walked him down to St. Peter Street, pointed out a house, and told him that was where we lived. Of course it really wasn't — I just told him it was. As soon as he went in I tore out for home, told my aunt what I had done, and begged her to go back with Uncle Ernest. She thought that maybe she ought to in order to get me out of that bad neighborhood, so we all moved up to Sixth and Willow Streets.

Another musician I had met about this time was a Creole named Buddy Petit; he was a cornet player, one of the best, but also a very heavy drinker. (His stepfather was Joseph Petit, a valve trombonist.) Buddy was working at the Tuxedo Dance Hall, on Iberville between Basin Street and Franklin.[2] This place was in the district that was later called Storyville. Buddy asked me, "Lee, why don't you go down in the District and play? You're a tall boy anyway, so all you have to do is just put on some long pants."

[2] Lee probably intended to locate the Tuxedo Dance Hall on Franklin between Iberville and Bienville.

One evening in 1915 I got word to go to the corner grocery store where all of us in the neighborhood always took our telephone calls (not many people around there had their own telephones in those days). It was Buddy Petit's wife, asking me to work in his place that night because he was not going to be able to make it on account of his drinking.

I was some proud! I put on Uncle Ernest's boxback suit and perched his Stetson hat on the back of my head. Then I left early for downtown — too early, in fact, so I had to sit around waiting until the place opened up. Then the boss called to me and wanted to know what I was doing there. So I told him that I was going to play cornet there in place of Buddy Petit. He looked at me and laughed, then he said if I didn't get out of there as fast as I could go he was going to call the police and get me sent to Jones's Home.

Well, I left brokenhearted — first, because I was not going to get my chance to play, and second, on account of having taken Uncle Ernest's suit and Stetson hat without his permission. The funny thing about my outfit was that I also had on a pair of high-button shoes and long-ribbed black stockings. But I thought I was the hottest thing in New Orleans. In spite of the disappointment about not getting to play, I stopped on the way home and had my picture taken. In those days boys wore short pants, and you had to be twenty-one years old before you could put on long pants. But I had not reached my fifteenth birthday yet.

After I got my picture made I went to Jack Carey's place. Ernest "Punch" Miller, Louis Keppard (Freddie Keppard's brother), and Johnny Dodds was there. Johnny lived just around the corner from the club. He told me he was going away with the Billy and Mary Mack show and that if I was not so young he would have taken me with him instead of Robert Taylor, another trumpet player.

There was a piano in this place, back of the saloon. The musicians would go back there to play, and the cornetists had cutting contests. Now, I was nothing but a kid, so when I went there it was to listen and learn something.

I also did a lot of rehearsing with young bands coming up. There used to be a fellow named Peter Davis who had a band in Jones's Home, and he used to get boys off the street, to keep those kids away from wild parts of New Orleans, and practice them and teach them. But this same Peter Davis used to take other boys in a lot, too. We used to go back to his home and practice all day long, and sometimes all night.

Mardi Gras time was coming, and they were short of musicians. One day a drummer named Black Benny[3] met me on Rampart Street and said, "You little son-of-a-gun, Lee, I hear you're gettin' real good on that cornet, so I want you to play a parade for the Zulus' Club on Mardi Gras Day." He gave me a dollar deposit to make sure that I would show up for the job like I was supposed to. Benny told me to be at the Zulu Club by nine o'clock. Louis Armstrong and another boy, Louis "Kid Shots" Madison — he played cornet too — were there also. These guys were very good, of course, so that was a proud day for me.

Later, George "Pops" Foster, the bass player, came after me one day to play in the Eagle Band at a dance that was going to be given in Nelty Hall at Josephine and Robertson streets. Bunk Johnson, their regular cornetist, was off on another one of his famous drunks. I told Pops I didn't think that I was good enough yet to play with them, but really I was so excited to think that I would get the chance to work in that great band. Pops told me not to worry, that I would be with the best ragtime band in New Orleans — and this was true. One thing in my favor was that I knew all the standard numbers like "High Society" and "Panama" and, of course, the blues. So when the time came to go to the dance, Pops called for me and promised my Aunt Mabel that he would look after me and see to it personally that I got home okay after the job. In fact, he said he'd bring me home himself.

After the first number I played with the Eagle Band that night, the boys started telling me that I sounded like Bunk, that I had the same tone and the same kind of feeling he had. Now, Bunk Johnson was my idol; he was the best jazz musician when I was a boy. Of course, there were many others who blew plenty of cornet in their own ways, but Bunk was way ahead when it came to jazz — I'm talking about hot phrasing, not trick tone or trick effects. It was said that he took his style from Buddy Bolden, so this

[3] Black Benny Williams, who is identified in Chapter 3.

style came from Bolden, through Bunk, to Buddy Petit, Louis Armstrong, and me.

Speaking of Bolden, I am sorry that I never got to hear him; I was too young when he was sent to East Louisiana State Hospital, a mental institution, in 1907. But I went to school with his son Charlie, a tall, nice-looking fellow like his father. I saw a picture of Buddy Bolden that Jimmy Johnson, the fine bass player, had. Jimmy played in Buddy's band and would tell me about him. Charlie Bolden told me a lot about his father, too.

My aunt and uncle left New Orleans in 1917 to go to work at Muscle Shoals (a dam and power development on the Tennessee River about thirty miles upstream from Florence, Alabama). They heard that there was plenty of money to be made there. I was left with my Aunt Esther and her husband, a man who was known as Mootsey, but I was really on my own.

At the Illinois Central Railroad station they had a sign that advertised for help wanted to work on the railroad up north, with passes given for transportation. So Mootsey and some others decided to go, taking me along with them. I put on some old clothes and packed my best suit in a paper bag, never dreaming how far we were going. I found out the next day, though. Everyone except me had brought a lunch, but no one, not even Mootsey, offered me any. The third day, when we got to Cairo, Illinois, I was pretty near starved.

When the gang would be sent out to work, I wasn't able to do any regular labor on the rails on account of being only fifteen years old, going on sixteen. So the boss set me to tightening bolts, but when he saw that I was no good at that, either, he made me water boy. After a month was up we had a payday, but they held back two weeks' pay on us.

Me and a boy by the name of Skinny McGraw used to go out in the woods and climb apple trees, waiting until the whistle blew the time to go to dinner at the camp. We always got breakfast before leaving camp.

One day a white boy passed by, and he happened to have a cornet with him, so I asked him to let me play it. He gave me the horn and I begun blowing the blues, just thinking about New Orleans. The work gang stopped working and started in to dance. I made up my mind then to leave the camp.

So me and Skinny McGraw caught a train for Chicago — that is, we thought it was for Chicago. Somehow we got separated, and I ended up in Bloomington, Illinois. I went to a boarding house run by a man named Curly Shields, and he said that his rooms cost seven dollars a week. Now, I had never heard of a room costing so much; in New Orleans we only paid seven dollars for a whole house. Besides that, I was dirty and didn't even have a change of clothes because my only suit had been stolen. Shields wanted to know if I could wash dishes and work around a restaurant. I told him, yes, I could, so he gave me a clean shirt to put on.

I went for a walk through town and met a woman named Bessie; she was about twenty-five years old, I guess. She took me to a dance, but they wouldn't let me in, so Bessie went in alone. I crashed the dance anyway — when the doorman turned away for a second I sneaked in. The band was swinging "Alexander's Rag-time Band"; that was a favorite tune at the time. I made a beeline for the bandstand and asked the leader if I could play something with them, but the musicians only laughed at me, and I heard someone say, "That tramp, he can't play nothin' at all." Just then the doorman spotted me, but I pleaded with him and said that I was only a young cornet player from New Orleans. So he told the leader, "Let's see if this young tramp can blow something," and the cornet player handed me his horn.

The leader stomped off "Alexander's Ragtime Band" again, and I came in right after the second chorus. I went into the third chorus, standing there with my eyes shut, playing and thinking about dear old Rampart Street. When I finished and opened my eyes again, everybody was crowded around the bandstand, stomping and hollering, women trying to kiss me and men hugging me. After that I started driving down some mean old blues for them.

In the meantime, Bessie was strutting around and telling the other women to lay off me, that I was her man. That sounded funny to me and made me stick out my chest, because I was only just starting my sixteenth year. Bessie wanted to know where I was staying, and I told her, then she asked me to go to her room and live with her. That night she gave me twenty-five dollars, so in the morning I went out and bought me some shirts and pants.

Now, Bessie was what they call a "payday woman" — I mean, she would go to the railroad camps on paydays. I stayed with her about three months. I also timed the trains, and one day, while she was off on one of her "payday trips," I bought a ticket and lit out for Chicago. I didn't know anyone there except Joe Oliver and a few other New Orleans musicians, so I went to the Pekin Cabaret, where Joe was working, but the doorman wouldn't let me in. (At that time Joe Oliver had Roy Palmer, trombone; Lorenzo Tio, clarinet; Tony Jackson, piano; and Minor Hall, drums.) Not getting in at the Pekin, I went around to 35th and State streets where Sidney Bechet and Freddie Keppard were playing at the Deluxe Cafe, but I couldn't get to see anybody there either, so then I went to 29th and Dearborn streets and got a room for the night.

The next morning I bought a railroad ticket for Cairo. I gave a Pullman porter ten dollars there, and he smuggled me onto the Panama Limited. I only had twenty-five cents left when I got back to New Orleans and took the Louisiana Avenue car for home. Aunt Mabel and Uncle Ernest were there, and they wanted to know where I was and what had happened to me. But I only told them that I had gone away to work up North, so they let it go at that. I crawled underneath my bed, pulled out "Old Betsy" — that was my cornet — and warmed her up some.

Earl Humphrey and I made up a teenage band. In it we had John Casimir on clarinet, his brother Joe on drums, "Barrel House" Bob Smith on guitar, Lib Newton on bass, Earl Humphrey on trombone, and myself on cornet. We played for house parties for fifty cents a night. We were all in our teens.

I was getting pretty fast on my cornet. One night I met a famous trombone player by the name of Jack Carey. He had heard us play and gave us a job playing for a white fraternity house. The job paid seven dollars a man. I had never made that much money in my life before. I got up and made a speech saying, "Boys, we are getting someplace and are pretty good. We should break up and go with older fellows."

I remember one Labor Day when Louis Armstrong and Buddy

Petit and me played a Longshoremen's parade. Everybody was dancing in the streets, and when we came down St. Charles to Canal Street we three cornet players made everyone stop and listen, because there was plenty of jazz! The mounted police stopped the band because we were playing so barrelhouse and all the people, white and colored, were cutting up so bad. So the police told us to let the crowd cool off awhile.

Those street parades were where New Orleans musicians made their reputations in the jazz world! Later on I used to play a parade practically every week because I belonged to two or three brass bands. Two or three men made up the brass we had. Practically every orchestra had a brass band; they would hire different musicians and form a brass band. The most famous brass that I worked in was the Tuxedo Band, led by "Papa" Oscar Celestin. That was always the top in my time — that really knocked me out. We used to play funerals practically every day and street parades for different clubs.

I ran into Pops Foster in the street, and he asked me, "Are you still playing cornet?" Pops said that Tig Chambers had gone to Chicago, then he asked me to come and join the Columbia Band in Tig's place, which I did. The Columbia Band had lots of work and played for all the rich parties out at Audubon Park. I was the only kid in the band. I crossed over from the Columbia Band to another band they called the Golden Leaf Band. It was managed by Jessie Jackson (a guitar player), and it was an up-and-coming band. A very good cornet player by the name of Zu Sullivan had got killed at that time, and I took his place in the Golden Leaf. I played with the Golden Leaf Band for about a year.

Then I joined Jack Carey's band. During intermission on a job one night the boys in the band went out to smoke and have a drink, leaving me on the bandstand because I was too young and they wouldn't give me anything to drink anyway. (I have to say that in those days the older musicians took better care of the younger ones than they do today.) One of the waiters passed by and asked me why I wasn't out with the other musicians taking a little nip. I just smiled, but he went and gave me a bottle of gin. I gulped it down like it was water, getting drunker and drunker all the time. The first thing I did then was to loosen up the bass violin, and next I loosened the snare drum, put match sticks in the mouthpiece of Jack Carey's trombone, and unscrewed the guitar. I had just got done with all this deviltry when the men came back to play. Zeve, the clarinet player that was leading the band,[4] stomped off a tune, but no sounds came out. I was the only one playing like nothing had happened; they raised Cain, but I acted real innocent.

Because I had worked with the Columbia Band and all, I began to get quite a bit of recognition from other musicians as being from the Buddy Bolden and Bunk Johnson school of playing. But Arthur Williams, a clarinet player, told me that I would not be able to play in the better type of places unless I changed my style. About this time I got the chance to work with a blind clarinetist who sounded something like Sidney Bechet. Also in this combination was Fred Miller, trombone; Irving Joseph, drums; Little Dad Jones,[5] a banjo player that looked like a midget; and T-Boy, bass.[6] The original cornetist with the band was Wesley Dimes; he later went to Baton Rouge, Louisiana, where I heard he did good and had a good business, but he got killed there somehow.

Big Eye Louis Nelson, a great clarinet player, quit Freddie Keppard and the Original Creole Orchestra in New York in 1917 and came back to New Orleans and took a job playing with Buddy Petit at Economy Hall. One night Buddy got dead drunk and was sound asleep when the time came for him to play, so some of the musicians tried to get me up on the bandstand to take his place. Not knowing Big Eye at that time, I was afraid to go and ask him to let me play, but I finally got up enough nerve. Big Eye wanted to know if I could really play cornet, saying that if I couldn't not to touch that horn. I told him I could play and that I knew all the standard tunes, including "Panama." So he stomped off on that and I really tore it up.

When we finished, Big Eye said he had had his eyes shut and that it sounded to him like Bunk had slipped up on the bandstand instead of me. Then he asked me what my name was, and I told

[4] Probably Zeb Lenares.

[5] Probably Clarence "Little Dad" Vincent.

[6] Collins may be referring to another musician here, for the most well known New Orleans musician with the nickname "T-Boy" in those times was a trumpet player, Dominique "T-Boy" Remy.

him I was Lee Collins. So then Big Eye asked me if I knew Oscar Collins from across the lake; he was surprised to find out that Oscar Collins was my uncle. Big Eye said that my Uncle Oscar was a great friend of his and that they used to go across Lake Pontchartrain together and eat oysters. He said that Oscar Collins was a great trombone player.

Next door to us lived a young girl who was a piano player by the name of Lillian Spillers. She worked at a well-known Carrollton joint run by an Italian called Tony. Every morning Lillian and me would meet up in front of her house. At first, I didn't pay too much attention to her; the only thing I did was bow to her and then she would bow to me.

One morning I arrived home from work and found Lillian standing in the door, talking to my aunt. They were talking about me, and my aunt was telling Lillian that I had not made my seventeenth birthday yet. That got me very angry, as I was such a big boy for my age that I always let on to the girls that I was older. In fact, I had told Lillian I was twenty-one. Lillian thought that my aunt was my mother and that she was just putting my age down to make herself look younger.

At that time I already had a girl friend, Louise Daniels. She was a very nice girl, and her parents were very strict. Her father was a longshoreman. I used to go to visit Louise but would run away when I saw her father because he had such a thundering voice.

One night I called to see Louise. Around nine o'clock, her father came into the parlor and told me, "Young man, it is time for you to leave. Louise has got to go to bed now." I got out of there as fast as I could; I knew that Louise was a good girl. Once I asked her to go to a show with me, but instead of going there what I really wanted was to take her to a rented room. She soon put me in my place, telling me that we were young yet and had plenty of time for that sort of thing after we got married. I never bothered Louise again after that. If I was once refused, my policy was to forget it.

Jack Carey hired me one night to play at St. Catherine's Hall. This was a Catholic hall and one of those high-class places, so the priest there didn't allow any ragtime music played. We began at eight o'clock and were supposed to quit at midnight, but the priest stopped the music at ten o'clock because he said it was too jazzy. It was then that I began to believe that maybe I did play too barrelhouse for places like that. I worked with Jack Carey until 1919, playing at Spanish Fort, Bucktown, Milneburg, and all around town.

The first time I ever laid eyes on Lulu White, the big "madame" from the District, was when I was out to Spanish Fort. She would go there and bring along all the girls that worked in her famous Mahogany Hall on Basin Street. Of course, all the pimps would be at Spanish Fort, too. Although she died a pauper, Lulu White was a great tipper in those days; we knew we stood to make a lot of money any night she would come to hear us play. Now, the pay was not much, but the musicians made a lot of tips because all the "madames" would vie with each other to see how much money they could spend in the different cabarets. Lulu White was a large woman, weighing over two hundred pounds. She had thick lips — it was rumored around that she went to Paris to have them cut down, but I don't know if this is true or not.

Other famous "madames" besides Lulu White were Josie Arlington (she was before my time) and Countess Willie V. Piazza. Her house was at 317 Basin Street. Willie was not from New Orleans, like many people thought; she was from Jackson, Mississippi. All her family was mulattoes.

I played a dance one night across Lake Pontchartrain. In this band I had Joe Lindsey, drums; Lorenzo Tio, Jr., clarinet; Bob Lyons, bass; and my father's brother, Oscar Collins, trombone. Uncle Oscar sat on the bandstand, tears rolling down his cheeks. I wondered what was wrong with him, crying like that, and he said it was because he was so proud of the way I had improved on my cornet. He told me he wanted me to stick with my music always.

About this time Lillian Spillers, the girl piano player next door, and I fell in love. One morning when I met her I noticed she was crying, and she looked so unhappy that I kissed her and asked what was wrong. She said we had been going together for a long time, and she felt that if I really loved her we ought to get married. I was the happiest boy in the world when she asked me to marry her. But on account of being underage, I couldn't get a marriage license. So that night I asked some of the older musicians to see if they could get the license for me, but they refused and were very much displeased about the idea of me getting married, saying I didn't know what I was doing. But I was lucky; I finally got Arthur Williams to get me the license. Lillian and I had many a fight. She didn't want me to talk to any of the girls that worked in the places where I was playing.

One night we went to the Bulls' Club. You had to be one of the best musicians to work there. My reason for not playing at the Bulls' Club was that I grew up Uptown, and they didn't think I would be good enough, as none of them had heard me play. Anyway, Kid Ory and Louis Armstrong were supposed to work at the Bulls' Club the night I am speaking of, but they walked out due to some misunderstanding or other. Jerry Reed, president of the Bulls' Club, asked me if I could get a six-piece band together for him, so Ernest Kelly, a trombone player, and I did that. The crowd carried me all around the place when we played there the first time. After that night I had it made for dances at the Bulls' Club.

I will never forget when I signed the contract to work there every Tuesday night. Lillian said, "Old man, it looks like you are goin' up in the world now."

2

New Orleans — the Twenties

I left Jack Carey in 1919 and went in a band at West End with Zutty Singleton, Big Eye Louis, and a piano player named Tink Baptiste. This band was known as "the jazziest four in New Orleans." We stayed together until 1920, and then Zutty and I moved to the Cadillac with Albert Nicholas and Udell Wilson.

Later that year I went to work at Morris Moore's "black-and-tan" cabaret located at Gasquet and Liberty streets. It was the only black-and-tan in town and was very high class. This place was once run by a big white pimp named Barney Moore, but he was before my time. The band that I took into Morris Moore's cabaret was Frankie Duson, trombone; James Williams, clarinet; Henry Zeno, drums; and Johnny King, a great piano player from Mobile, Alabama. I was copying Bunk Johnson's playing to a "T," and Morris Moore was very fond of me.

Now, Morris Moore was a big-time pimp himself. He wore a big diamond on his finger, a diamond horseshoe stickpin in his tie, and plenty of fine clothes. I told Morris one night that I wanted to be a pimp like him. "Lee, stick to your horn," he said, "it is God's gift. In the first place you would probably fall in love with one of them whores and then you would be a trick, and a whore hates a trick like God hates sin. Next thing, she'd have you blowin' your horn night and day to make more money for her, then maybe stick a knife in you." Morris said, "Look at me; I don't care nothin' for a prostitute. I have a fine girl, I just bought her a mink coat, and she gave me a diamond ring that cost about two grand. Some day, when I'm ready to settle down, I'll marry her." That was a good lesson he gave me, it made me see life as it was. I am glad now that I kept to music and music only!

Morris Moore also told me the story of Clerk Wade, a tall, good-looking boy who came to New Orleans from Memphis when he was very young. Wade was square as a brick but looked good in his clothes. He started out hopping bells in the hotels around town. But some whore took and turned him into a pimp; she bought him diamonds and fancy clothes and gave him money, too. Then, early one day this same trollop came into a place called the Big "25" Club and shot poor Clerk Wade dead.

The Big "25" was a gambling den, but on the side they had what you might call a little cook shop where all the musicians, pimps, hustlers, and prostitutes would go in the early morning for their griard (a kind of veal dish), biscuits, rice, and coffee. There was a big stain on the floor of the Big "25." Some said it was Clerk Wade's blood. Anyway, it would never come off.

I'll never forget the Saturday night gig that I played at a place called the Brick House in Gretna, Louisiana, just across the river from New Orleans. This was a tough joint run by an Italian fellow. I was working there with a bass player named Duck Ernest Johnson. Out at the Brick House there was a woman known as Copper Wire. She kept treating me to fish and potato salad and also all the drinks I wanted. Later, she put five dollars in my hand. Duck Ernest saw this and warned me not to talk to Copper Wire because she was a tough woman and no good, so I took his advice and quit talking to her. Soon a pretty Creole girl by the name of Rosa came in. She went for me. The next thing, I saw Copper Wire going into her bosom and pulling out a long switchblade knife. I jumped out of the way just as she made a pass at me and the blade went clean through Joe Lindsey's thirty-dollar hat. Joe was the drummer; he was also one of the New Orleans fancy boys. I left the Brick House and took the ferry back to New Orleans.

Right after that I played a job for Butcher Hill at a place

Uptown that he called Butcher Hill's Lawn Party.[1] We worked there three nights and were paid good money because the place was packed all the time. In the outfit I had at Butcher Hill's was Eddie Vinson on trombone; Big Eye Louis Nelson on clarinet; Lorenzo Staulz, guitar; Bob Lyons, bass; and Joe Lindsey, drums. The boss used to call me "little Buddy Bolden" when he saw how I would talk with all the girls that came there.

I remember the Sunday night Butcher Hill got killed. He had just left his house and was walking into the place. I heard five shots and then someone said that Butcher was dead. He was well liked, and in no time there were policemen from all the precincts all over the place. They questioned everybody, but no one ever found out who it was killed him. Now you talk about a funeral! Butcher Hill's was the biggest I ever did see.

After that we took a job at the Battle House in Mobile, Alabama. That band was Big Eye Louis, Bob Lyons, and Lorenzo Staulz, who were with me at Butcher Hill's place; Maurice French, trombone; Edna Francis, piano; and Black Happy Goldston, drums.

We went to a rooming house on Davis Street. Each of us had made some money and transportation, so we decided to shoot some dice. Black Happy, who stammered when he talked, got down on his knees and said, "D-d-dice, if you ever was a f-f-friend help me now. This is my last d-dollar." But he threw big craps, or "boxcars," as they are called, and I won the payroll from the band.

While we were passing through Bay St. Louis on the way back to New Orleans, there was a man at the railroad station selling stuffed crabs. I bought all that he had, and we had ourselves a real feast. When we got back home Black Happy told me he was broke, that I had won all his money, and asked me to loan him two dollars of his money. I gave him five.

That was a very good band we had in Mobile, but every guy in it — and the one woman — had eyes for cabareting; no one wanted to travel anymore. So we broke up. Edna Francis went in a band with Louis Armstrong, Big Eye Louis joined the John Robichaux band, and Black Happy got a job with Oscar Celestin. I

[1] Al Rose and Edmond Souchon, *New Orleans Jazz: A Family Album* (Baton Rouge: Louisian State University Press, 1967), p. 210, give "Butchy Hill's," Protection Levee at Oak Street.

went to another band with Zutty Singleton, Udell Wilson, a guitarist named Willie Santiago, Willie Jackson, and Nooky Johnson, who was doing the singing. This band played at the Cadillac for about a year.

All of us musicians used to go to a place called Sweet Child's, at Gravier and Franklin streets, where we would drink gin and absinthe. Waiting for us there would be Ann Cook, a fine blues singer, and other people like Mary Jack the Bear, Good Pussy Virginia, Gold Tooth Irene, and One-Leg Horace.

One New Orleans character I can't forget was Bucktown Bessie, hostess at the Cadillac, where I worked. She got her nickname because of hanging out at a place in Bucktown, a tough resort on Lake Pontchartrain. Bucktown Bessie was an awful gold digger, but she got big tips for us from the customers. On top of that, she would often send out to fancy restaurants for the musicians' dinners.

Later in 1920 I went to visit my father across the lake at Gulfport; Lillian and I were on another one of our spats at that time. While over there I decided to go to Mobile and get with a band. Jelly Roll Morton's cousin, a real Creole boy that spoke more French than English, was on drums; Arthur Bond was the guitar player; a boy called Acey, from Mexico, was on bass; and a Japanese fellow was on clarinet. We left Mobile and went to Hattiesburg, Mississippi, where we stopped at a restaurant run by a Greek fellow on Mobile Street. I took my cornet out and we started playing; in a few minutes the place was packed and jammed, with people coming from everywhere. We were doing so good there for a while that I sent for Edmond Hall — after he came, the Japanese boy switched from clarinet to trombone. The white people didn't want the Japanese to play with the band, but he wouldn't leave us, saying that he got more feeling out of the music that we played, and he could really swing.

The boys from Mobile left and went back home, but Edmond Hall and I stayed in Hattiesburg and got up another band. With us this time was a piano player called Jug Shaw and also another one by the name of Coonie Vaughans. Coonie never left the South but always stayed around Hattiesburg. He was a piano player from his heart and could also fake a little on trombone, so he wanted to play trombone with us. We toured all over the South. Coonie got too much to drink one time in Knoxville, Tennessee, and decided to kill himself. So he fired away but only managed to shoot himself in the foot. That put him out of operation for a while. He was well liked around Hattiesburg and would even go to the mayor's house late at night to get his whiskey money when he was broke.

After that band broke up, Jug Shaw and I went to Selma, Alabama, but the band we organized there didn't make out too good, so we decided to leave and try our luck in Birmingham.

Jug and I shared a room in Selma, and before we could get to Birmingham we had to try to figure a way to get our luggage out of the boarding house without the landlady seeing us. We were broke and couldn't pay our rent. (One reason some of us musicians liked to rent in private homes was that the few hotels there were in the South at that time generally weren't fit to live in.) We decided to throw our luggage out the window and then slip out the door. So Jug tossed his stuff out the window and made it down to the station. Then I sailed mine through the window, too — only it seems like it hit the landlady right on the ear. By the time I got out of the house, she had grabbed onto my bag and wouldn't let me have it. I pleaded with her and said that I was broke and hungry and was trying to get to Birmingham to find work and that I would send her what I owed as soon as I got a job.

"All I get from you musicians and show people are sad stories," she said. In a way it was a chance that landladies had to take in those days, because it's true that sometimes entertainers would get stranded in different places and there was no way of getting their money. Anyway, she finally let me go. When I got down to the station, Jug was on the train waiting for me. I was a few pennies short on the train fare, but the conductor let me on. We got to Birmingham and went straight to the Frolic Theater on Eighteenth Street where they booked all the big T.O.B.A.[2] acts.

I told the theater manager that I was a cornet player from New Orleans and was looking for work. He said to stick around, that in case one of the acts didn't show up — and if I really could

[2] Theater Owners' Booking Association.

30

play — he'd put me to work that week. As it happened, Jack Wiggins, a great tap-dance star, did fail to show up, so the manager, good to his word, went on stage and announced that Wiggins could not get there but that he had a man that claimed he played cornet. Now, I didn't even get a chance to rehearse with the pit band, but I went out on the stage anyway and told the musicians that I was going to play "Home Again Blues," which was sweeping the country at the time.

Those cats hit a big introduction, and I closed my eyes and started blowing. The house was in an uproar when I finished; the pit band was standing up looking at me, and a girl ran up on the stage and threw her arms around me and kissed me. I had to cry when I got back to the dressing room. Just a few hours before I was broke and hungry, and now I was king! I stopped all the shows. The manager came to me and said that if I wanted to I could play with the pit band regularly. I told him later that I wanted an advance on my salary, and he gave it to me, saying I could have anything I wanted.

I had a line following me that night when I left the theater. I went to where Jug Shaw had found a job playing at the Elks Club. I sat in with him awhile, then we went to a good-time house where a piano player named Cannon Red was playing the blues. He was a great blues man, and I played my cornet with him, too.

After working in Birmingham for a while, I went back to New Orleans. Lillian was still acting up, though, so in 1921 I accepted an offer to go to Pensacola, Florida, for Prince Morris, a dance promoter who was also an undertaker. I took Earl Humphrey, trombone; Edmond Hall, clarinet; Albert Morgan, string bass; Joe Strater, drums;[3] Caffrey Darensburg, banjo; and a Pensacola girl pianist named Sadie who Morris hired for me there. We worked two jobs, one for Morris and the other at the Naval Aviation Station.

One Sunday I had the toothache *so* bad and could not get to a dentist, so I drank whiskey all day, trying to stop my tooth from hurting. I couldn't play when I got on the job, so Edmond Hall, who didn't drink at all, bawled me out for getting drunk; he knew that I never used to get drunk before.

[3] Probably Joe Stroughter.

The Pensacola job did not last long. Edmond and Al Morgan decided to stay in Pensacola, but Earl Humphrey and I went back to New Orleans and joined Buddy Petit's band at the Bissant Dance Hall up in Carrollton. I blew first cornet because Buddy liked to play second. I loved this barrelhouse bunch, as Petit was such an idol of mine, but the band broke up pretty soon, so I went to work with Jack Carey at an after-hours place where the people had to have a key to get in. This place was for all the sporting people and gamblers. One time the boss's sister threw me a note saying she wanted to meet me after I finished playing, but the boss got the note when it fell on the floor. So the boss told the bass player, "When you get off work tonight you get another cornet player. This boy plays good, but the girls go for him too much!" I sure did hate to leave that job, though, as there was good money in it.

After that I went with Sidney Arodin, a fine clarinet player and a fine man, in an all-white band. This was at a hole-in-the-wall place on Decatur Street run by a Spanish pimp who was a swell dresser. This guy had about seven women working in his place. One of them was known as Sis, but for various reasons I can't call her real name. In those days there was a tough New Orleans police captain named Smith. One night he came into this joint, so Sis warned me that if he asked any questions about me working in this white band I should tell him I was Spanish in order to avoid trouble.

Sidney Arodin and I were crazy about stuffed peppers, so after we got off from work we would go to the French Market, buy them by the dozen, and walk down the street eating. Sidney loved to go down to the river and sit for hours, just watching the water. I happened to have my cornet with me there the time that he was making up "Lazy River," so I know I was the first musician to ever play that tune.

After I left the place on Decatur Street, Sidney would stop by where I was playing and sit in with me. Sometimes he got so high that he would not go on his regular job. But I liked him and his playing so well that I had him to record with me later on the Jones-Collins Astoria Hot Eight sides for Victor.

Another job I had was at the Orchard, on Burgundy Street, with Albert Nicholas, clarinet; Luis Russell, piano; Roy Evans, drums; and Willie Santiago, guitar. After a while, though, we went back to where we had been playing at the Cadillac and were re-placed by Louis Armstrong, Zutty Singleton, Udell Wilson, Johnny St. Cyr, and Barney Bigard. Louis's job at the Orchard didn't last long, either.

I'll never forget the time that Andrew Foster took a baseball team and a band out on the road. In the band were Maurice French, trombone; Tom Benton, banjo; Bob Lyons, bass; Joe Lindsey, drums; and myself. Now, Andrew Foster was also doing a little bootlegging on the side. When we got as far as Jackson, Mississippi, he gave Joe Lindsey and me his grips to hold. Mississippi was a dry state, so two policemen came up and told us to open the grips, but we said they didn't belong to us, they belonged to Andrew Foster. So he had to open them. Quarts and half pints of whiskey came rolling out and went every which way all over the ground. Poor Andrew got hauled off to jail, but he had a lot of friends in Jackson and was soon released. I was young and always ready and willing to travel as long as I could blow my cornet, but I had enough of that tour!

So I went back to New Orleans and kept on working with all of the city's great musicians — except for Mr. John Robichaux, who was a very high class musician. He was the most respected musician among both white and colored, and his orchestra played for the white society dances. But most Negroes didn't care for his music; it was more classical.

Well, Mr. Robichaux came to Francs Amis Hall with some high-class Creole friends of his one night when I was playing there with Jack Carey. I don't think anyone was more surprised than I was when he spoke to me, saying, "Hi, little Lee." I didn't think he knew me at that time. But seeing that he did know who I was after all, I went over to him and said, "Mr. Robichaux, I sure wish I could play in your orchestra, if nothin' else but second cornet."

"I would like to have you with me, little Lee," he replied, "but you play such barrelhouse cornet that I don't think you would fit in very well at the places where I work." So I didn't get a job.

Mr. Robichaux told me that he was sitting there listening to me and that he said to Barney Bigard's father, "Now, there is a boy with a beautiful tone; he is between Buddy Bolden and Bunk Johnson, but he dishes it out so hot." He asked me if I had ever heard Buddy Bolden play. I said I was too young, but that I had heard Bunk. Then I wanted to know what kind of a man was Bolden, and Mr. Robichaux said that he was a guy something like me and that he played ragtime cornet and was the greatest of all the cornet players. Every musician, of course, had great respect for Mr. Robichaux, and you can bet that they sure were looking at him talking to me.

Punch Miller and I were in Buddy Petit's band one time on Mardi Gras day; we were playing for the Zulu Club. Louis Armstrong was working on the steamer *Capitol* with Fate Marable then, but he was on the "second line" all that morning. Louis asked Punch to let him play in his place. So there was Buddy Petit, Louis, and me, all blowing like everything; when we hit Rampart Street we were really jumping! I was the youngest in the bunch, and they got quite a kick out of my playing.

Punch left New Orleans later on and went to Chicago, playing with different bands there — Erskine Tate and then Frankie Franko's group at the Golden Lily, a Chinese restaurant on 55th Street.[4] That was about 1930. Punch also worked with Fate Marable, but that was before he went to Chicago.

After most of the great cornet players had left New Orleans — Freddie Keppard, Joe Oliver, Louis, and Tig Chambers — the only ones left there were Buddy Petit, Henry "Kid" Rena, and myself. So the Zulus gave a dance at National Park, which was at Third and Claiborne Streets, to choose the king of the cornet players. They had all three of us there, but I won the silver cup. They carried me all over the park.

In 1923 I was working at the Suburban Gardens, the biggest gambling place in New Orleans. With me there was Zue Robertson on trombone; May Neeley, a girl from Shreveport, Louisiana, and a very fine piano player; Duck Ernest Johnson, string bass; John Marrero, banjo; Alphonse Picou, clarinet; and Red Happy,[5] drums. Jack Dempsey came in one night, and in his party was a guy that

---

[4] The latter group is probably François' Louisianians, given as working at the Golden Lily in the early thirties in Paul Eduard Miller, "Thirty Years of Chicago Jazz," *Esquire's 1946 Jazz Book* (New York: A. S. Barnes, 1946), p. 10, and in Miller and George Hoefer, "Chicago Jazz History," *ibid.*, p. 34.

[5] Red Happy Bolton, who is further identified in Chapter 3.

threw silver dollars to the band. The rest of the musicians got insulted and went to the back of the place, but I stuck around and caught about twenty dollars. We stayed there at the Suburban Gardens for maybe about a year. Then I went with Chris Kelly, a trumpet player.

In 1924 Joe Oliver sent me a wire from Chicago, saying that Louis Armstrong had left and that he wanted me to join his famous Creole Jazz Band at the Lincoln Gardens. Before that, Joe had written a letter to Lorenzo Tio, Jr., asking him about the best cornet players down there in New Orleans, and Tio told him I was about the best jazz cornet player in town. In fact, Tio wrote back and said I was blowing my ass off.

When I received the wire from Joe Oliver I could hardly finish reading it, I was so proud and happy. I told Lillian I got a chance to go to Chicago with Joe Oliver, and she said, "What? How about me? What do you think about me going?" We both walked around in a daze for about an hour before we could say anything. Then I made a beeline right for Western Union and sent Joe a telegram to tell him I would like very much to come to Chicago and join him.

I left for Chicago on September 1, 1924, and met Joe and the band at the Lincoln Gardens, 459 East 31st Street, near Rhodes Avenue, for my first rehearsal. The Lincoln Gardens (which was known as the Royal Gardens before that) was a big place and had an upstairs balcony. There was a large crystal chandelier that hung from the middle of the ceiling. They had a spotlight shining on this chandelier so that reflections would play on the people as they danced around on the floor beneath. The personnel of the Creole Jazz Band after I joined were Joe Oliver, first cornet; myself on second cornet; George Filhe on trombone; Junie C. Cobb, clarinet and saxophone; Stomp Evans, alto saxophone; Diamond Lil Hardaway, piano;[6] Bud Scott, guitar; Bert Cobb, bass and sousaphone; and Clifford "Snags" Jones, drums.

[6] Lil Holloway is given as Oliver's pianist in 1924 by Walter C. Allen and Brian A. L. Rust, *King Joe Oliver* (Belleville, N.J.: Walter C. Allen, 1955), p. 15. However, Diamond Lil Hardaway recorded with Vocalion in 1928 and Decca in 1936. Collins also names her as the pianist with whom he worked in Chicago in 1931 (see Chapter 4).

Of course, I had a lot of butterflies in my stomach and was very nervous when I made my first rehearsal with Joe Oliver. This was because I had so much admiration and respect for him. At the rehearsal Joe said, "Lee, for your benefit we are going to open with 'Panama Rag,' " and then he stomped off. That band really swung up a breeze, and Joe told me to take some choruses. So I did, and the more I would blow with those guys the better I would get — I did blow some that day! After rehearsal Joe telephoned his wife, Mrs. Stella, to tell her that he was bringing Lee Collins home to dinner.

I really felt at a disadvantage the first night I played with the Creole Jazz Band at the Lincoln Gardens, because Louis had made such a great hit that no one thought he could be replaced. Joe called "King Porter Stomp" for the opener, and then "Panama." Everybody gathered around the stand to find out what I could do and see if I was going to be able to make it in that band. There was Arthur Rhoades, he was Jack Johnson's nephew; Bud Red, the manager; King Jones, the master of ceremonies; an ex-fighter named Roy Williams, who was the bouncer; and Walter Thompson, a Chicago policeman who came from New Orleans and had been a musician himself.

Joe was all smiles after we finished playing the first set. Roy kidded him and said, "Joe, this is the first time I seen you smile since your boy Louis left the band," and Arthur Rhoades said that Louis and me sounded just alike to him. "That's Lee Collins, my little Creole boy," Joe laughed. He said we wouldn't need any rehearsal the next day, that I was okay.

Walter Thompson wouldn't leave the place that night until we played "High Society," but Joe told him we couldn't — that we didn't have a New Orleans clarinet player. So I said I would play the clarinet part, that Lorenzo Tio had taught me how. I remember when I first started playing, "High Society" was a very popular tune. It was really a test for the clarinet players, and when I found that many of the young clarinet players couldn't cut Picou's solo, I decided to learn it on cornet. By listening to Picou, Johnny Dodds, and others play it, and with Tio's help, I got so I could play every note. Then when I'd play in a band that had a weak clarinet player who didn't know or couldn't play Picou's solo, I would play it on the cornet.

After we played "High Society" at the Lincoln Gardens that night, Joe grabbed and hugged me. Joe Oliver was a fine man. He gave all the cornet players a chance to show what they could do and was not jealous of his musicians.

The Lincoln Gardens caught fire on Christmas Eve of 1924. I remember that everyone was scrambling to save their overcoats, and someone took mine. In the mix-up it was my good luck to get hold of a brand-new Melton. It was a beautiful coat, and I know that someone must have got it for a Christmas gift. This was fortunate for me, because when I arrived in Chicago I only had what you might call a "tissue paper" coat, it was so thin, and you can imagine how I suffered when the weather got real cold. That winter was one of the coldest there had been in Chicago in a long time.

After the fire, Joe told me to stick with him, saying that he was going into the Plantation Cabaret on 35th Street. In the meantime Lillian gave birth to a baby boy. We had saved our money, and Lillian was worrying me to go back to New Orleans. She finally did go home, but I decided to stay in Chicago awhile longer. I did not go into the Plantation with Joe Oliver, though.

When I was working at the Lincoln Gardens I ran around some with Jelly Roll Morton, and he talked to me about making some records with him. So one day I went over to see him about this at his room at 35th and Grand Boulevard (now South Parkway). There he was — in bed with two women, one sitting on each side of him. I tell you, he was some character!

Jelly wanted to know was I going to stay in Chicago or run on back home like a lot of other New Orleans musicians did. Then he asked me to come to work with him. "You know that you will be working with the world's greatest jazz piano player," he boasted. I told him I knew he was one of the greatest jazz pianists, but he said, "Not one of the greatest — I am *the* greatest!"

Jelly finally got dressed, and we went in his car to see the manager of a big-name ballroom out on the South Side. But he and this man could not come to any agreement on the price Jelly wanted for playing there. He told the manager, "You bring Paul Whiteman out here and pay any price he wants because he has the name of 'king of jazz.' But you happen to be talking to the real king of jazz. I invented it and I brought it here." Jelly was a peculiar man — if he liked you he liked you too much, and it was the same way if he hated you. He was also very prejudiced and liked nothing but Creoles.

I finally did make some records with Jelly Roll. They were on the Autograph label, and we recorded in the old Lyon and Healy Building. In the group that recorded we had Roy Palmer on trombone, Balls Ball on clarinet, Jelly on piano, and, of course, me on trumpet. Roy Palmer was an old friend of mine. I never heard of Balls Ball before we made those records, and I never saw him again afterwards. I don't know where Jelly got him from, but he played "High Society," so I think he must have come from New Orleans originally.

The tunes we recorded were "High Society," "Weary Blues," "Tiger Rag," and "Fish Tail Blues." The last number was mine, but I never received any credit for it. Jelly took that number from me and later recorded it as "Sidewalk Blues." When I went back to New Orleans and saw an orchestration come out of "Sidewalk Blues" and played it on down once, I saw it was my own number, the number I had been playing around New Orleans so many years. Roy Palmer warned me not to play it until I had it copyrighted, but I didn't take his advice. All I wanted to do was make the record. It was my first one.

Besides Jelly Roll, another New Orleans pianist that was around town in those years was Arthur Campbell. He came to Chicago with Freddie Keppard. Campbell was a little before my time, but I used to hear all the old-timers in New Orleans talking about him. One night while I was still working with Joe Oliver I happened to be passing an after-hours place on 35th and Prairie Avenue where Keppard was playing. Freddie was doubling two jobs at that time; he also worked at Harmon's Dreamland out on the West Side. Freddie spotted me going by this place and wanted me to go upstairs and play a set for him while he finished talking to some friends. When I got to the bandstand, I found that I didn't know any of the musicians except the clarinet player, Jimmie Noone. I found out that the other guys were Arthur Campbell and Ollie Powell, who was the drummer and singer — he could really sing, too. After we finished the set Campbell told me he didn't have to ask where I was from — he knew by my horn that I was a New Orleans man.

During the 1920's many people out on the South Side held parties to help pay that high rent — house-rent parties, they were called. Every place that would have these parties was furnished with some kind of piano. All the pianists played boogie-woogie and blues and stomps. House-rent-party piano players or anyone else that could play would get paid for playing and also would get all the liquor they could drink. A bunch of us used to go to one of these flats for a drink sometimes after getting off work in the morning. The landlady would serve gin in a cream pitcher, but it would cost a dollar and a quarter if you wanted ginger ale with it. First, she would serve you a drink, and then everybody in the place had some of your gin, so that the pitcher was empty when it got back to you. Then you'd have to buy some more in order to get even one good drink.

In those days, I remember, the Chicago Police Department had a big yellow Cadillac that the cops roved the South Side in. One morning I was standing on the corner waiting for a taxi. I whistled like mad at what I took at first to be a Yellow Cab, but when it rolled up and stopped where I was I could see it was that big yellow squad car. As he got out of the car one of the policemen asked me, "When did you get back in town, Curly?" And the other one wanted to know what was the last time I had been arrested. Then I realized that they had mistaken me for somebody else, so I told them my name and that I had only just come up from New Orleans to play with Joe Oliver's Creole Jazz Band. The reason I answered to the name Curly was that my hair was curly, so some people really did call me that.

During the short time I was in Chicago, about six months, I got so many letters from Lillian begging me to come home that I slipped out of town one day and went back to New Orleans. That was about March of 1925. After I got back I was very popular among the musicians and owners of the different cabarets because I had been up in Chicago playing with the great Joe Oliver. I had but to name my job.

I went to work in a four-piece band at the Entertainers Club, the old 101 Ranch, and stayed there over a year. We had Udell Wilson, a very good piano player, George "Georgia Boy" Boyd on clarinet, and Ernest Trepagnier on bass. We were the talk of New Orleans and packed every night. The guys from Fate Marable's band used to come and sit in — Charlie Creath and lots of others. Things was going good, and I was feeling fine. I didn't miss Chicago at all, because I was back home where the jazz is played like I like to hear it, and everybody was playing so good.

The manager at the Entertainers then was Morris Smith, a well-known pimp who was called Chinee because he had hair and eyes which looked Chinese. Chinee was a tall, handsome mulatto, and he dressed in the latest of fashion. He always had a cigarette in a long, gold-tipped holder, a gold toothpick in his vest pocket, a diamond stickpin, and diamond cuff links. The fashion at that time was that men had monogrammed belt buckles, too. Chinee had only taken this job to be doing something, which was not much, and to meet new girls, who he would make if he could. You can guess the results after they started going with him! Such men had a way of baiting those poor girls in by buying them all kinds of beautiful gifts.

After I went back to New Orleans from working with Joe Oliver, it was Chinee who introduced me to Albertine McKay, a beautiful woman from the District. She had been Freddie Keppard's girlfriend when he was playing there. This woman caused me untold trouble and almost cost me my life.

No sooner had I started going with Albertine than she took over my life and demanded respect — you would have thought we were married twenty years the way she acted. She was at the Entertainers every night to see that I went home with her after work. Some of the musicians said that she was going to kill me some day, the trouble I had with her — and it pretty near worked out that way, too.

One day I got full of gin and absinthe and told Albertine that the next Thursday was my birthday. I only said this for a joke; I didn't think she would take it serious. But Albertine asked Manuel Manetta, a musician who was also an agent for Werlein's music store, what he thought she should get me for a birthday present. Manuel told her to buy me a trumpet because all the cornet players were switching to trumpet then. So she had Manuel to pick out a trumpet for me, and they kept it hid until that Thursday night.

At midnight the bartender called me over to the bar to get a drink, and he and a guy that we called Pork Chops sang "Happy Birthday" to me. I'd forgotten all about that joke I had played on Albertine. Then it came back to me what I had done — here it was only June, and my birthday would not be until October 17!

The bartender asked me to play "Oh, How I Miss You Tonight," so I went to the bandstand to get my cornet. But there on my chair was this beautiful new gold-plated Buescher trumpet. I picked up the trumpet and started to play; I was very proud of it. Albertine kissed me and said, "Happy birthday, darling."

After that night she really did take charge! She was so jealous that the musicians didn't want to even talk to me if she was around for fear she might think they were giving me a message from some other girl. I could not keep my mind on my music with some jealous woman around. I was a man who wanted to be free to play on my job — that was one reason, too, that Lillian and I didn't get along too good. And I had a habit of calling all the girls "sweetheart."

One night some girl came up to the bandstand to give us a tip for playing a certain song for her. Albertine had gone out to get a bottle of gin and a frog loaf for me, and she came back just in time to see the girl leave the bandstand. Albertine threw the bottle at me, but her aim was bad and it hit Georgia Boy right on top of the head. Gin went all over the place. Then Albertine threw the frog loaf out in the street.

Another time I went to the monte table to watch the game. Also standing there were two girls, and I was in between them, but I didn't know them from Adam; they were perfect strangers to me. Albertine came in and saw me next to the two girls. She grabbed me and tore my shirt almost off me. I was so mad I could have killed her; we really did shake the place up. Johnny Lala, boss of the Entertainers, barred Albertine from there after that.

After I quit going to Albertine's house she would be out front of the Entertainers waiting for me, but I used to slip out the back way and go home to Lillian. One night Albertine sent word to me that she wanted to see me out in the street. The bartender warned me that she was going crazy and most likely would kill me on sight. But I went anyway. Albertine asked me why I didn't come to her house any more, and I told her I was through and to quit bothering me. Then suddenly she came up with a big .38 pistol and started blazing away at me. The only thing that saved me was a post that I ducked behind to wait until she had emptied her gun. The street was full of people, I remember. When I went back inside, Johnny Lala, the owner, told me to take off for a while. He was afraid that Albertine would kill me there and get his place closed up.

So I went scouting around the District for another job. It happened that a big gambler was in town from Dallas, Texas, and was looking for a band and some Charleston dancers. I talked this deal over with a dancer and master of ceremonies named Sherman "Professor" Cook — he was the one that later invented the Lindy Hop. At this time he was working at the Hummingbird Cabaret but not doing so good. Figuring to get away from both Albertine and Lillian, I told Cook not to tell anyone but that I would get up a band for this gambler. I hired Freddie "Boo-Boo" Miller, trombone; Henry Julien, saxophone and clarinet; Big Gaspar, violin; Octave Crosby, piano; Irving Joseph, drums; and Caffrey Darensburg, banjo.[7] We went to Dallas and worked for a man by the name of Son Lewis who had a roadhouse and gambling place. After finishing work there each morning we would go out to Riverside Park and play from two-thirty until four o'clock.

I guess I was not satisfied with getting out of woman trouble in New Orleans — I had to go and get mixed up with a Dallas girl. She was the type that carried one of those long Texas jackknives and just dared me to look at anyone else.

Someone told Lillian that I was in Dallas, so she called the police there and they found me. She was telephoning me every night, and I finally decided to go home, though I did hate to leave, because we were making plenty of money. After I had gone back home, the boss fired Professor Cook, thinking that somehow he was

[7] The photograph of the band in Dallas shows the personnel as listed by Collins except that there is no violinist in the photograph, and Percy, not Caffrey, Darensburg is the banjo player. Also, the drummer may be Arthur Joseph or he may be Coke Eye Bob (as identified by Danny Barker).

the cause of my leaving. All the boys left the band except Caffrey Darensburg and Irving Joseph.

As I recall, I went back to work for Johnny Lala at the Entertainers. Albertine had gone to Chicago while I was away, because someone had told her I was up there. On account of what had happened before, and because there were so many women following me, Lala was afraid someone would kill me, so he hired a bodyguard for me — a tough man named Poole. Before Poole would let anyone come near me he'd find out who they were and what they wanted, and even then he watched at all times. No one would take a chance on this man. In later years Poole was killed by Eddie Scott.

There was a guy named Beansie Fauria that ran a place called the Creole Fantasy. It was in a good location, right next to the Lyric Theater, but business was very bad at Beansie's place at this particular time. So Big John Evans — that was the bartender at the Creole Fantasy — told Beansie that the Entertainers was packed and jammed because of me playing there. All the show people from the Lyric Theater were going to the Entertainers, and with all those celebrities you could hardly get in the place. Big John wanted Beansie to try to hire me for the Creole Fantasy, but Beansie said that asking Lee Collins to come there would be like asking for Johnny Lala's eyetooth. Beansie had had Udell Wilson and Ernest Trepagnier in the band at his place, but they quit and joined me at the Entertainers.

One night while I was on my intermission, Beansie stopped by and asked me how I was doing. Then he offered me a big price to come and work for him. I told him, "Beansie, I never run out on a man or do him any harm unless he do me some." However, I did talk Beansie's proposition over with Udell, and he said my musicians were with me; whatever I wanted to do was okay with them. So we did not go to Beansie's place. My going to Chicago had changed everything — after I left Joe Oliver's band I didn't know my own power.

Then Big John left Beansie's place and came to work at the Entertainers. Big John — he was nicknamed that due to weighing close to three hundred pounds — was one of the New Orleans bartenders that came in for their share of popularity right along with the musicians. He always mixed drinks and named them after the people he made them for; of course, it had to be someone of note. He made a special drink for me once, calling it "Lee Collins" instead of Tom Collins. Big John liked jazz bands, and he was used to all the greats.

After I had been back home from Dallas awhile I joined Eddie Jackson, the bass horn player, in a band under the leadership of Oscar Celestin. We went to work at the Music Box at Canal and Carondolet, but I didn't stay with them too long.

Later that year — that was 1926, I believe — I made up a band of Creole musicians and went back to Pensacola, Florida, taking Lillian along with me. This band consisted of Ernest Kelly, trombone; Arthur Derbigny, alto saxophone; Lee Rezuan, tenor saxophone and clarinet;[8] Joe Robichaux, piano; William Lebouf, drums; James Desvigne, bass; and Danny Barker, Paul Barbarin's nephew, banjo.

I must tell you about Danny Barker; he was around sixteen years old at the time. I was working Downtown and saw Danny playing a ukelele out in neutral ground on North Claiborne Street. He was known as the "ukelele king." Danny was dressed like a New Orleans pimp and had on a pair of Edmond Clapp pointed-toe shoes. I asked him if he had ever played banjo, and he said no, so I took him to Werlein's music store on Canal Street and bought him a banjo. In a few months he was one of the best banjo players in New Orleans; he stayed with me until he left for New York. Danny later worked for Cab Calloway and a lot of other bands, but my band was the first one he ever played in.

Every Creole man in New Orleans, even if he was a musician, learned some kind of trade. Some were plasterers, and a great many of them were cigarmakers. For musicians, of course, this would only be a second trade. In the early days, some Creoles, even the ones that had Negro blood, sent their children to schools in France. Or, if they were not sent to Paris, they went to the white schools. I am talking now, of course, about those with fair skins and straight hair. The Creoles were very strict in their homes, and their morals were high. They were also prejudiced to the dark-skinned Negroes.

[8] Possibly Joe Rouzon.

44

When I was a young man in New Orleans, you could cross the old Basin on Marais Street to St. Peter Street and then you would be in the old Treme Market on Orleans Street. There you'd see the Creole housewives out shopping in the early morning with their baskets on their arms and bidding each other the time of day in French. They all preferred speaking French to English. Tonti, Laharpe, North Derbigny, Dumaine, St. Ann, and many other Downtown streets — that was Creoleville, the home of Freddie Keppard, Sidney Bechet, Jelly Roll Morton, Manuel Perez, and a lot of other jazz greats. Today, though, you won't find but a few real Creoles around there. A lot of the old ones are dead now, and the young ones have crossed over to the white side. And there is no more open Treme Market.

I remember the time when I went down to Arnold Depass' home at Annette and Villere Streets for a rehearsal with the Olympia Band. They had been trying to get me to come with them, saying, "Lee, why don't you leave from Uptown and come down here with the Creole musicians?" So I decided to go and play with them. The Olympia Band at that time consisted of Big Gaspar, trombone;[9] Albert Nicholas, clarinet; Willie Santiago, guitar; Albert Glenny, bass; Arnold Depass, drums; and me on cornet.

I took a girlfriend named Mazie with me to the Olympia Band rehearsal. Now, she looked like one of the Creole girls, but she made some bad mistakes; the first was that she went to Depass' home with her face made up and with lipstick on. Then, besides that, she sat down, crossed her legs, pulled out a cigarette, and began to smoke. The old ladies that were there started jabbering away in Creole and giving us a bad look. Finally, Arnold Depass' mother-in-law told me that Mazie would have to go out in the back yard if she wanted to smoke, because there were children in the house. After lunch I played one more number with the band and then we left.

Mazie was introduced to me by a trumpet player named Kid Harris. She was a nice girl and did not drink. I went with Mazie for quite a long time and promised I would divorce Lillian and marry her. But as time went by she began to realize that I didn't really mean to get a divorce, so one day she drank a big bottle of iodine. I called a doctor in, and he sent her to a hospital to be pumped out.

[9] Probably Vic Gaspard.

45

I was scared to death; I thought that the policemen were going to arrest me.

But that passed over, and Mazie and I still went together. After taking the iodine, she was not feeling very well, so I suggested that she ought to go to the Touro Infirmary to get a check-up. So one day she did go, but it had to be our luck that Lillian happened to be there, too. They did not know each other, but they struck up a conversation, and Lillian told Mazie that she was married and that her name was Collins, too — she had noticed that Mazie went by that name. Lillian then said that her husband was a trumpet player and that he worked at the Entertainers. That was one time it was good that Lillian was quite a talker, because otherwise Mazie might have said that her husband was Lee Collins and all hell would have broke loose. It would have been bad for Mazie, as Lillian was a pretty good fighter in her day. I went with Mazie for a long time, but then I gave her up because I knew I was not going to divorce Lillian — not at that time.

But one day when I was out drinking with the boys I got to thinking about Mazie and decided to go to her house. I was pretty drunk when I got there. I remember her trying to tell me something, but I couldn't understand what it was. Somehow she finally managed to put me to bed.

That evening when I woke up, Mazie told me she wanted me to meet her husband, and she called him in and introduced him to me, saying, "Honey, this is Lee Collins that I told you about." He was a nice man to come home and find me in his bed and drunk. He offered me some dinner and went out and bought a drink for me, and he also took me home. I felt so ashamed for the way that I had acted. After that, I never bothered her any more. Mazie was always afraid of me, and she knew that I carried a big .38 Colt with me all the time and would not be afraid to use it.

In 1926 I organized my own band for the Club Lavida, on Burgundy Street in the French Quarter. We stayed there until into 1928, if I remember right. With me I had Big Eye Louis Nelson, clarinet; Earl Humphrey, trombone; Joe Robichaux, piano; and John and Simon Marrero, two of the Marrero brothers, on guitar and bass. There was a big family of Marreros, and they all played one kind of stringed instrument or another.

Later in 1928 I was playing with my own band at the Astoria Gardens, on Gravier Street near Rampart. The name of the band was Collins and Jones. In the band was Davey Jones, who played tenor sax and mellophone; Nat Story, trombone; Big Eye Louis Nelson, clarinet; Theodore Purnell and George Washington, saxophones; Joe Robichaux, piano; Roy Evans, drums; and Danny Barker, banjo. Before Danny came in, I had Emanuel Sayles on banjo. That was a band!

While talking about the Astoria, I want to say something that a lot of books and writers forgot to mention — and that is the fact that the Astoria Hot Eight was my band! And how we came to go to the Astoria was that Davey Jones had a job there but no band. I was working at the Lavida, and Davey came to me and wanted me to take the job with my band, so I promised him I would. Then Beansie — he was boss of the Astoria at this time — went ahead and had posters made, and we went out on the truck, advertising that my band would open up at the Astoria. I went to my boss at the Lavida and told him that I was leaving, but somehow he talked me into staying. So I told Davey that I wouldn't take the Astoria job after all. The next night Beansie came to see me and said that if I didn't work for him I wouldn't work any other place in New Orleans, either. So that is how I took the job at the Astoria.

Now, I wouldn't be telling this story right if I didn't say some more about Davey Jones, a very underrated musician. With all due respect to Joe Oliver, Davey was the one that polished me up on my music. Davey could teach and play any instrument, but he was just like a rolling stone — he never stayed any one place for any length of time. He played on the riverboat with Fate Marable, Baby and Johnny Dodds, and Louis Armstrong. While I was working in the District, he would come and sit in with my band and play any instrument that he picked up. One night I talked him into bringing his mellophone with him. I never heard so much mellophone barrelhouse playing before in my life. It was that night — this all happened long before the Astoria job — that Davey told me, "Little Lee, you sure have got some drive, yourself."

After he left Fate Marable, Davey joined Joe Oliver out in San

Francisco and then went into the band of Louis Humphrey, Sr.,[10] in Hollywood and did a lot of motion picture work. That was during the silent film days. He left Humphrey and came back to New Orleans and married a very popular chorus girl by the name of Lena Leggett; she was working with the Ethel Waters show. He opened up a school and taught a lot of musicians to read, since a lot of them were playing by ear. About this time was the beginning of the Astoria Hot Eight band.

A Mr. Pierre of Victor Records asked us to make some records, as this was a good band.[11] We were going to cut the records in a Canal Street music store, but there was some kind of mix-up, so the recording session was in an Italian dance place on Esplanade, where parties were held. We used Sidney Arodin on clarinet for the records instead of Big Eye Louis, our regular clarinetist, and Nat Story, the trombonist with the Astoria Hot Eight, never did show up, so he wasn't on the records.

Finding names for the numbers we recorded for Victor was easy. "Astoria Strut," of course, was named for the place we were playing at, and we called another tune "Damp Weather" because it was raining that day. The way the saxophonists took the breaks together gave us the title for "Duet Stomp." And "Tip Easy Blues" came about because Theodore Purnell would beat his feet when he was really tipping. "Purnell's tippin' easy," the guys in the band used to say.

The musicians would eat there at the Astoria at night, and when payday came they would pay their bill. When Danny Barker came into the band he began ordering all kinds of expensive dinners, and I wondered why he always asked for such big meals. The rest of us would order gumbo or sandwiches but not big steak dinners. One night Beansie asked me, "Who is this Danny Barker? I have a thirty-dollar tab of his here and he never pays his bill." So I went to Danny and told him that he owed for his meals that he had eaten. Danny said that he didn't think he had to pay as he had not seen

[10] Lee probably is referring to Willie E. Humphrey, who was active in New Orleans and California as a musician and who also worked in motion pictures in Hollywood.

[11] This could be a reference to Ralph Peer, who visited New Orleans as a talent scout and made recordings about this time for the Victor Talking Machine Company.

any of the other musicians paying anything. You can be sure that Danny was very careful about what he ordered from then on.

One thrill I remember was the night that P. G. Lowery came to the Astoria. Lowery, who was from Cleveland, Ohio, was with the Barnum and Bailey shows and was known as the greatest cornet soloist. He could make C over high C like it was nothing at all; he was the greatest of all time. The way he blew made goose pimples come over me; I had never heard a cornet player like him in my life before. Lowery was a fine-looking man and had come out of Tuskegee Institute — where I always wanted to go and would have if my grandfather had lived longer. Bunk Johnson told me once that he worked under P. G. Lowery and that he went with the circus on a tour of Europe. I don't know if that was true or not, as Bunk did a little stretching of the truth from time to time, but I do know that it was a great thing for all the musicians to listen to Lowery when he came to New Orleans with the circus.

An important part of New Orleans music was the custom for musicians to advertise the places they played and drum up business at their dances by piling into trucks or wagons and playing their best numbers while they drove through the streets. There were a lot of clubs in New Orleans, and they used to give dances on Sunday and Monday nights. Some of them would advertise on a Sunday for a Monday, and some would advertise Sunday for the dance that night. If a grocery store or a dry goods store opened up, they hired a band that day. We played funerals; we played street parades; we played for a lot of parties and other affairs.

So quite often there would be a lot of bands out playing in the streets, and that's how sometimes we would come to have fights or cutting contests. Sometimes two rival bands, both of them out advertising, would happen to meet at a street corner, and then there was a battle of music; there would be a competition. The band that played the best would have the dance on that Sunday or Monday that would get the biggest crowd. That's where you came to be popular and came to be called "the King." If my band played "High Society," the other band would play "High Society"; if we played "Panama Rag," they got to play "Panama Rag"; if we played the blues, they played the blues. We repeated the same tune to see who played the best. And if we came with a number, a terrific number that they couldn't follow, and they had to play something else, they lost and had to go away. There were real rules to those battles.

The cornet player, or the leader of the band, tried to get the reputation of being "the King," to be the best. And the band that had the King was the best and got all the work. One time Kid Ory was the King. He had the top cornet player when he had King Oliver, and after Oliver left, Louis Armstrong took his place. They would always win, and every place in town had Kid Ory's name up because he had the top cornet player. When Louis left Ory, Buddy Petit's band was in the field, and once he caught Ory and gave him a whipping. Ory felt he was no longer the King in New Orleans, and he hit for the West Coast.

It was a great thing in New Orleans. Everybody was trying to be the best, to be the King. But to be the best you had to work hard and to fight for it. And then everybody would be after the top man. They would go where he was playing, and when he was through playing they would get their horns out. They didn't take their horns out just to come help him play; they would take their horns out to try to carve him. They wanted to see if they could beat him playing, and if they did, they took over and became the King. Many times when a player became the King, New Orleans lost him. When he stepped out and said, "Well, I'm the King of the trumpet players," or "I'm the King of the clarinet," or the drums, or the bass, he caught a train and he'd be gone. He always had some guy that was next to him, and that man would take over.

A little before I left for New York I was out playing an advertisement with my Astoria band. That was my last advertisement in New Orleans. As it happened, Kid Rena was out advertising for the Lady Baby Dolls. When we got to the corner of Thalia and Freret, someone said that Rena's bunch had just left there, so at my orders, we went looking for them — I had my reasons, as I will explain. We found Rena and his band farther uptown with a big crowd around their truck. So we pulled up alongside and then we led off at him with my number, "Astoria Strut." Right away the people forgot all about Rena and started screaming for us. We run Rena's band off the corner. But before he left there, Rena climbed down out of his truck and told me I was too smart. He wanted a fight, but I wouldn't give him one. I reminded him of a time many years before when he caught me the same way and didn't show any mercy.

That happened one Sunday when Buddy Petit and Frankie Duson had a band for advertising and were running all the bands off the corners. This Sunday I was out advertising for the Zulu Club. Being the youngest cornet player, I was passed by because Buddy wanted to give me a break. After he left we ran upon Kid Rena and Georgia Boy Boyd. Buddy Petit had just given them a good whipping, so Rena decided to take it out on me because I was the youngest. Of course, he beat us pretty bad. So the time in later years when I caught up with Rena near Thalia and Freret was my chance to get back at him and settle an old score. I made the most of it!

3

The Musicians

The last year I played regular in New Orleans, though I did go back for visits from time to time, was 1929. In 1930 Luis Russell sent down for me to join his band at the Saratoga Club in New York, but before I tell you about that I want to stop my story and pay tribute to some of the great New Orleans musicians that I knew and worked with during those carefree years.

Some of the top New Orleans cornet players, besides Buddy Bolden, Bunk Johnson, Joe Oliver, Buddy Petit, Freddie Keppard, and Louis Armstrong, were Manuel Perez, Henry "Kid" Rena, Louis Dumaine, Tig Chambers, Punch Miller, Henry Allen, Sr., Sam Morgan, Joe Nicholas, Robert Taylor, Oscar Celestin, Wesley Dimes, Andrew Kimball, Willie Edwards, Tommy Ladnier, Thomas "Mutt" Carey, Amos Riley, Chris Kelly, Louis "Kid Shots" Madison, Joe Johnson, Chief Mathews,[1] Guy Kelly, Henry "Red" Allen, Jr., Maurice Durand, Frank Keeling,[2] and Peter Bocage. These are the cornet players that helped to make the city of New Orleans known as the city of jazz.

Tig Chambers was a powerful cornet player. He was a tall,

[1] Lewis "Chif" Matthews.
[2] Given as "Frank Keelin" in Al Rose and Edmond Souchon, *New Orleans Jazz: A Family Album,* p. 66, and as "Frankie Keeley" in Paul Eduard Miller, "Fifty Years of New Orleans Jazz," *Esquire's 1945 Jazz Book* (New York: A. S. Barnes, 1945), p. 11.

dark-skinned, handsome fellow and quite a ladies' man, too. Tig played the Buddy Bolden style. He couldn't read a note of music, but he had a beautiful tone and played real barrelhouse.

Tig went to Chicago before World War I to work for Bill Bottoms at the Dreamland Cabaret. I don't think that any of the musicians in Tig's band could read too much, but they could really play fine jazz. It worked a hardship on Tig, not reading, and Bottoms had to let him go because the band could not play the Dreamland's shows. (In those days Dreamland and other Chicago cabarets had shows that were big productions.)

After he lost the job at Dreamland, Tig's band took a job at a wide-open place called the Dusty Bottom, at 33rd Street and Wabash. Tig had Roy Palmer on trombone; Joe Robichaux, piano; and Snags Jones, drums. Roy tried to teach him how to read music, but Tig had been playing by ear so long that it was a waste of time.

Tig didn't do himself any good by leaving New Orleans. If he'd stayed there people would have heard about him. As it is, though, no one remembers him anymore except a few old-timers and New Orleans musicians. Tig Chambers died in Chicago in 1950 at the age of about seventy.

Buddy Petit was one of my real idols, and I'm sorry he didn't do any recording. I learned a lot from him. He played more like Bunk in Bunk's early days than anybody else. In fact, he was the King when Bunk got burnt out and went back to the country, to New Iberia.

Buddy had a big, round, beautiful tone and a lot of ideas, and he played with a real barrelhouse beat. He didn't play many high notes, but he didn't need to the way he played the lower and middle parts. A lot of times Buddy and I worked together as first and second cornet. He was a great second cornet player, which in some ways was harder to play than first. You had to have a good ear and be able to improvise and follow the first cornet anywhere he went. Buddy was also a great soloist.

I remember one night when I was playing at the Entertainers and Buddy came in. He was a very sensitive guy, and he wasn't doing so good — about burnt himself out on whiskey. He hadn't heard me since I got back from playing with Joe Oliver. I asked

Buddy to sit in and play a bit, and he didn't play so well; he sounded like a different cornet player altogether. So, I hated to turn him down, but I had to tell him, "Buddy, I'll come back and play." Buddy just sat on the bandstand and looked at me, and he made me start drinking and I got drunk. Because he made me feel bad, he started crying. He said, "Lee, I'm so glad to see you playin' like that; you put me in mind of myself, like I used to play." I said, "Buddy, you play good yet. You still play good, Buddy." It was a sad night for me, and I'll always remember it.

Around 1920 I met Evan Thomas, a great cornet player and band leader from Lafayette, Louisiana. He led the Black Eagle Band. Evan never did get the recognition he deserved. I heard him play in New Orleans one night, and to me he even had Buddy Petit whipped — and that was blowing some! When I asked Evan why he didn't come to New Orleans and stay, he said that he had too much work in Lafayette and around the country. One thing, Evan Thomas knew more about Buddy Bolden than anyone in New Orleans.

Chris Kelly was another fine New Orleans cornet player, but he wasn't as great as, say, Louis Armstrong or some of the others. He had a different style from all the other cornetists; I have never heard any style anyplace just like his. Chris was a popular player for dances and had a big following. When he would play the tune "Careless Love" the people would stop dancing and just listen.

One time when Lent was coming on — and jobs were scarce for musicians during Lent — Chris asked me to work with his band on a date for the Bulls' Club. He had Earl Humphrey on trombone; Little Chester Zardis, bass; Zeb Lenares, clarinet; Roy Evans, drums; and Lorenzo Staulz, banjo. The men wanted me to take the band over, but Chris got real angry with me, so I quit. Chris Kelly was a tough man, and the musicians didn't like him because he liked to fight. One thing about him, though, was that he didn't stay mad long and would soon get over it.

I remember the time that me, Buddy Petit, and Chris were playing a parade for the Young Men's Olympians, the club that Zutty Singleton belonged to. Buddy came on the job drunk, and while we were parading down Dryades Street he wasn't blowing at all, just walking along holding his cornet. Chris told Buddy he

54

needn't play, that he wasn't going to get any pay anyway. Later on that evening Chris was getting weaker, and Buddy was sobering up and started playing like hell. So they patched up their difference, and Buddy got paid after all.

Besides being hot-tempered, Chris was a real character; he would come to work in a tuxedo suit with a blue work shirt and tan shoes. He was a nice-looking man and weighed about a hundred and sixty pounds or more.

Another good cornet man was Joe Johnson; he and Buddy Petit had almost the same style. But Joe died young.

I have to give it to Freddie Keppard as one of the real greats. He refused to make records until he was way past his prime, so the younger people did not get to hear the real Keppard. Freddie had the first jazz band to leave New Orleans and go on tour. That was in 1912.

Eddie Vinson and I went to see Freddie in 1932 when he was sick and near death, but he was in good spirits and talked very strong, recalling the old days, and it didn't seem like he was as sick as he really was. He told us that the last time he ever saw Buddy Bolden, they were bucking each other for an advertisement in front of the Big "25" Club. Freddie said he sure was glad to see Bolden leave the corner, as Buddy was some cornet player. Shortly after our visit Vinson telephoned me with the news that Freddie Keppard was dead.

One of the kings of the New Orleans cornet players was Kid Rena. He came in the days of the Waifs' Home with Louis Armstrong, and he was another one of my idols. It's too bad he drank so much and his lip gave out early. Rena had a most beautiful tone and a range which was more perfect than any cornet player's I ever heard. He could play the high register so clear and beautiful. In the early days he used to really cut me when we would meet on the corners advertising some club.

Ikie Smoot — he was pretty wild at one time — was another good New Orleans trumpet player, but he didn't follow up with his music. He was also at the Waifs' Home at the same time as Louis. Ikie left New Orleans later on and went to New York to live.

I remember that Ikie made his first trip back home in 1922

to visit his father and sisters and to look up some old friends. The main one he wanted to see was Louis Armstrong, but Louis had just joined Joe Oliver's band in Chicago. So Black Benny sent Ikie over to hear me at the Winter Garden, Gravier and Rampart, where I was playing in Jack Carey's band along with Edmond Hall. Black Benny told Ikie that I played just like Louis. Ikie asked me to have a drink with him, but I wasn't drinking, so instead I started playing some of the good old New Orleans numbers for him. Ikie said, "Lee, you won't be here long." Sure enough, two years later Joe Oliver sent for me to take Louis's place in the Creole Jazz Band.

Before Ikie Smoot left the Winter Garden that night he put his hand in my pocket and told me to see what I had. It was twenty dollars, which was a lot of money in those days. Ikie must have given away about a thousand dollars while he was in New Orleans that time. That is one thing New Orleans musicians will always do when they go home — they don't forget their old friends. Louis is like that, too.

Black Benny himself was a very popular musician and one of the best bass drummers in New Orleans. Louis came up under him. He was a big, very dark man who looked something like Jack Johnson, the prizefighter. He got a great amount of respect from policemen as well as from other people. At one time he was a pretty rough customer, but later he reformed and got married and settled down.

Now, all theatrical and show people have a pet superstition; mine was black cats. What made me believe so much in black cats was what happened to Black Benny. I was working at the Lavida at this time, and Black Benny was at the Lyric Theater. He would come to the Lavida and sit in with me sometimes after finishing up at the theater. One night me and Black Benny and all of my band decided to go over to Benny Harvey's saloon at Gravier and Franklin streets. All the show people used to hang out there, as everybody thought that Harvey had the best gin in town. Just as we got to Rampart Street, a big black cat crossed our path. I stopped dead in my tracks. "Boys, I don't like this," I said, "that cat had eyes like balls of fire. Let's turn around and go down Burgundy Street."

But they all laughed at me because I wanted to turn back just for one block. So we kept on going the way we were headed.

Benny Harvey's saloon was packed with musicians and show people. We were not there twenty minutes before Black Benny was fatally stabbed by a woman he used to live with. She got mad with him for some reason because he offered her a drink. Anyway, she had never gotten over his getting married and quitting her.

I was standing next to Black Benny when the stabbing took place. If I'd had any idea that this woman had a knife, I could have saved Black Benny's life. Or maybe he could have saved himself if he had gone to a hospital instead of hauling the woman away to the First Precinct. All the guys in the band admitted later that Black Benny might not have got killed if they had only listened to me. This happened pretty near forty years ago, but I still think there is something to the saying about a black cat crossing your path. Always turn around and go the other way!

Roy Palmer, to my way of thinking, is one of New Orleans' greatest trombone players. He could take the clarinet part of "High Society" and play it on trombone as good as any clarinetist. Roy was way ahead of his time. He was a little too modern for New Orleans back in the early days. He wasn't strictly on a tailgate style like Kid Ory; he could really execute on the trombone.

Roy worked in Joe Oliver's band in Chicago, but he had a bad habit that caused him a lot of trouble — sleeping on the job. That was because he would stay up all day teaching trombone lessons. Two of his pupils were Al Wynn and Preston Jackson.

Joe Oliver used to bawl Roy out for sleeping on the bandstand and warned him that Bill Bottoms, the boss, was kicking about it. So one night Roy went to work real early, about six o'clock, figuring to get some sleep before the job. He put two chairs together in back of the coat racks for something to sleep on. The band hit at nine o'clock — but no Roy Palmer. About one o'clock in the morning, when the band had already played two shows, Roy woke up and came crawling out from behind the coat racks. Joe Oliver started in hollering at Roy for not being on the bandstand. Joe said he couldn't understand how, if Roy was behind the coat racks like he claimed, he didn't hear the music, loud as it was. Roy said, "Joe,

I was the first man on the job tonight — if you don't believe me, you can ask Bill Bottoms." But Joe said that being there sleeping instead of on the bandstand was just like not being there at all — no difference.

Roy left Joe Oliver's band and went to work with Freddie Keppard at the Deluxe Cafe. Keppard had Sidney Bechet on clarinet; Lizzie Taylor on piano;[3] and Bill Johnson, Jelly Roll Morton's brother-in-law, on bass. Roy lived in Chicago for a long time and made many records. He played trombone on the Autograph records I made with Jelly Roll. I heard he became a church worker.

There were other good trombone players in New Orleans besides Roy Palmer and Kid Ory. Zue Robertson was one of the first great ones. He used to travel a lot with the circuses and with shows. Then we had Honore Dutrey. He played with Joe Oliver a lot and later worked for him in Chicago. Eddie Atkins was also very good, but he was more for reading music.

Sam Morgan had one of the good New Orleans dance bands. His musicians were Yank Johnson, trombone; Joe Watson, clarinet; T-Boy, bass;[4] and George Guesnon, banjo. They were all good, but Yank Johnson was the only one that was really outstanding. Morgan was a trumpet player, but not what you would call great. He did have a nice, sweet tone, though.

Yank Johnson and his brother, Buddy Johnson, were very good trombone players. They worked about 1912 with one of the best bands in New Orleans — the Superior Band with Bunk Johnson on cornet (no relation to Yank and Buddy); Big Eye Louis Nelson, clarinet; Peter Bocage, violin; Tom Benton, guitar; and John "Ratty Jean" Vigne, drums. Everybody was there when they said, "Superior Band at Economy Hall."

William "Bebe" Ridgley was not the best trombone player in New Orleans, but he was a good businessman. He managed the Original Tuxedo Band for Oscar Celestin from 1912 to about 1927. Now, the Tuxedo wasn't the best jazz band, either, but they had all the best work in New Orleans because they knew all the popular tunes of the day and fitted in for the people they played for.

Ridgley and Oscar Celestin had a falling out over a two-dollar

[3] Probably Lottie Taylor.
[4] See Chapter 1, note 6.

leader's fee, so Ridgley organized another Tuxedo Band. He came to see me about joining the new band, but I didn't like spot jobs — moving around from one job to another. I always wanted to work in the same place every night. When I turned down Ridgley's offer he told me, "Lee, you're making a big mistake. I can get you twice the money you are getting in cabarets." He said if he could just get Lorenzo Tio, Jr., and me to join the new band he would run Celestin out of New Orleans. Ridgley was particular about the musicians that played with him, so when he couldn't hire the men he wanted he quit the music game and went into a different business.

A big thrill that I had was playing a funeral once with a great cornetist named Manuel Perez. He was leader of the Excelsior Brass Band, the finest New Orleans had at that time. In this band was Mr. Perez; Maurice Durand, trombone;[5] Isidore Barbarin (drummer Paul Barbarin's father), baritone horn; Peter Bocage, alto horn; Ernest Trepagnier, bass drum; and Bebe Matthews, snare drum. My chest swelled way out to think that I was with these great men.

As I have said before, many of the great New Orleans musicians went to Chicago in later years. At one time Chicago looked just like New Orleans, with all the players from down that way. One of these men was Arnett Nelson, a clarinetist that worked with Jimmy Wade's band. Now, this was the first Negro band to leave Chicago and go to New York and play downtown. In this band was Eddie South, violin; a piano player by the name of Spaulding, who was very good; William Dover, trombone; and a great drummer by the name of Willie Jackson. Wade was the trumpet player, and Marie, his wife, a very popular cabaret singer in those days, was the vocalist.

Arnett went to Chicago around 1916 and has been there ever since. He was a great clarinet player but had a weird style, something like Wilbur Sweatman — real vaudeville clarinet, not my style of clarinet player. Arnett's biggest trouble was that he liked to do tricks with his clarinet; he would take it all apart and play it. He played at a very popular cabaret at 39th and Indiana, out on the South Side. Arnett played his very first job in New Orleans with my father's band after Lorenzo Tio, Sr., left.

[5] Maurice Durand was a noted trumpet player of the time.

59

All the best New Orleans musicians used to get a kick out of bucking each other. Baby Dodds and Red Happy, two of the greatest drummers of them all, came around once to where Zutty Singleton was playing and got into an argument about who was the best one. It ended with Zutty's drums getting torn up, but he told me that he couldn't really get mad about it because Baby and Red Happy were both such good musicians. Zutty was one I admired very much and still do today.

He was a character, too! I never will forget the time when we worked at the Cadillac in New Orleans. Our boss, a big-time pimp from the Vieux Carre, walked in with a beautiful suit on. Zutty was admiring it and asked how much it cost. The boss told Zutty that a suit like the one he had would cost too much for Zutty to buy, that he had paid a hundred and fifty dollars for it. At that time a suit costing that much would be like paying two or three hundred dollars for one now. But in a few weeks up popped Zutty with one just like the boss had.

Another one of New Orleans' great drummers was Snags Jones. In the early years he broke in with Buddy Petit's band and then played with all the other great jazz bands in New Orleans. He and Baby Dodds had the same style, only Snags could do more tricks than Baby. Snags was a drummer that could take eight sticks and juggle them under his arms and in his mouth and play all eight of them at the same time, also keeping time.

It was about 1921 when Tig Chambers sent for Snags to come to Chicago. Then he went to Milwaukee, Wisconsin, and worked on the Wisconsin Roof Garden with Bernie Young's Creole Band. Snags was with Joe Oliver's band twice, first on the road and then at the Lincoln Gardens. He played with Joe until the fire, and then Paul Barbarin came in the band. Snags played around Chicago with different bands and in later years joined Darnell Howard's group at the Bee Hive.

Snags was always worrying about my health in the late 1940's. The night of his death (in January of 1947) he telephoned me only two or three hours before he died. He wanted me to try to get Oliver Alcorn to play clarinet on a concert date that we had for that Sunday evening at Moose Hall. Later that night his wife called and told me that Snags had died. I could not believe it; then I broke down and cried. So another drummer, named Jerome "Pork Chops" Smith, asked me what was wrong, and I told him that the best friend I had in the world was dead. Snags and I went to school together when we was kids. I just couldn't get over his death. His body was sent back to New Orleans without any musicians attending his funeral or those in New Orleans even knowing about it.

All the drummers wanted to be like old man Louie Cantrell;[6] he inspired a lot of kids to play drums.

New Orleans had its share of blues singers and guitar players, but they had a different style than those from other places. One of them was Lonnie Johnson, who was very good and a very popular man at one time. On one of his trips back to New Orleans in 1925 he used to sit in with my band, playing his guitar and singing the blues. He stayed around town for about six or seven months that time. Years later he worked with my band out in Calumet City, and in 1948 we both joined Kid Ory's band to play in Carnegie Hall in New York and, later, Orchestra Hall in Chicago. Lonnie is not to be compared with the blues singers from, say, Mississippi or Arkansas; he has more jazz in his guitar playing and can swing with a band. In my book he is one of the greats.

New Orleans could produce anything for the asking when it came to music or blues singers. Another one who sang the blues like Bessie Smith and was known as the queen of the honky-tonks was Ann Cook. Ann was a very rough woman, but most all blues singers in those days were rough women. A lot of people used to ask Ann why she didn't leave New Orleans and go North, but she would say, "I'm doin' all right here, so why leave?" Later on, Ann stopped singing the blues and got religion. I don't know what finally became of her.

One of the most popular singers in New Orleans at one time was a guy by the name of Carey Fritz. He was a good dresser and was well liked by the women; he would sing songs just for them. He hung out at all the black-and-tan places that had the best jazz bands. In fact, a cabaret — such as Beansie's place at Iberville and Burgundy; Pete Lala's at Iberville and Marais, where Joe Oliver

---

[6] Also spelled Cottrell.

used to work; or the Entertainers at Iberville and Franklin — was nothing if they did not have Carey Fritz singing there. As soon as a woman came into the place he would meet her with a big smile and sit with her; later he would dance with her and sing softly in her ear.

Now, New Orleans had two race tracks, one at Jefferson Park and the other one at the Fair Grounds. When the jockeys, trainers, and clockers came to some place with their girls to cabaret a little, Carey Fritz would always find someone that was not spending money fast enough and would take their table away from them. He made forty or fifty dollars a night for himself. Carey would make a beeline to the bandstand and ask me to play "Poor Butterfly." When he finished his song he would sit at the table with some poor guy and his girl and sing to her "You Are My Everything." If Carey Fritz was still living he would still be popular because he kept up with the times. But he got killed in a car accident.

Speaking about singing, there used to be lots of guys around New Orleans that could sing real good. They got up quartets — my Aunt Esther's husband was the head of many a one — and would go around to some of their friends' homes to sing and eat and drink beer, or maybe it would be a cowein (a kind of turtle dish) dinner with plenty of wine to go with it. That was some of the most beautiful singing you would ever hope to hear. After everyone was drunk, the last song would always be their old favorite, "Sweet Adeline."

A lot of people have heard so much about Rampart Street and want to know what kind of street it is. Well, Rampart is like State and 35th streets in Chicago some years ago or like Wiley Avenue in Pittsburgh or John Street in Cincinnati. Rampart runs north and south. Starting at Howard Avenue Uptown is the beginning of the honky-tonks, barrooms, clothing stores, and pawnshops. Also, I must not forget all the greasy eating places that are called "cook shops."

Upstairs on the corner of Julia and Rampart was a tough place called the Red Onion, run by Vic Dubois. It was just as tough as Funky Butt Hall, where Bolden used to work. If you didn't play the kind of music the Red Onion customers liked, they would walk up to you and want to know if you were a Sunday-school teacher. I know, because many was the time I worked there as a kid; Buddy Petit would get drunk and send me in his place. There was Sidney Bechet, Clarence Williams, Frankie Duson, Lorenzo Tio, Alfred Williams, Red Happy, and the Marrero brothers John and Lawrence — they are just a few that played there.

The Red Onion was always packed with out-of-town women; it drew them like a magnet. As soon as they got off the Illinois Central train, they would walk across the street and go to the Red Onion. There were no chairs in the place to sit on, so they sat on wine and beer kegs. The first time I ever saw the game called Georgia Skin was at the Red Onion; it wasn't a popular game in New Orleans.

"You can cut the funk in this place with a knife," Alfred Williams used to say when we would go upstairs to start the job. The boss of the Red Onion knew the type of music to hire for his customers — and they knew their jazz!

One day Earl Humphrey and me went there to listen to the music. We had our horns with us, so we put them in back of the bar when we went downstairs and started drinking tokay wine. The Red Onion bar was on the first floor. Then we hit a lot of other joints down the line and wound up at the Astoria. When we got ready to leave there we remembered about our horns. When Earl was starting back to try and find them I told him, "Don't ask the bartender if we left them there — say we *did* leave them and now we want them back."

Earl came back to the Astoria in a little while and told me, "Man, you like to got me killed. The bartender in one place told me, 'you know you have not left no horns here,' then he said if I didn't get out fast he would knock my head off." So I told Earl to follow me, and we went back to Julia and Rampart. I ordered the bartender to hand me those horns that we left there, and he reached down in back of the bar and gave them to us.

The Downtown section of Rampart Street, which is to the north, has some residences, a few saloons, and neighborhood combination grocery stores–saloons.

Rampart is separated from Basin Street by the Southern Railroad and depot. From Canal to St. Louis Street and from Canal to Conti there were many little two-room cribs that were rented to the whores. These places had shutters and doors and windows where the women sat or stood, calling out to men as they passed by. If the men didn't want to go in or hadn't made up their minds, the women would decide for them by dragging them in off the street. The girls, dressed in short gingham dresses and Chinese slippers, would walk down the streets singing "Stack o' Lee Blues" or "2:19 Done Took My Baby Away." For a fact, all those women could really moan the blues. There have been harlots coming and going in New Orleans ever since the 1700's, when France sent over some women from the brothels of Paris.

The streets in the District were always crowded with the local boys with their fancy silk shirts, and, of course, there would also be sailors and whatnot off the ships docked in the harbor. The Black Maria was busy every night. You would hear some frail hollering, "Watch!" — that meant she was calling for the police to come and protect her. Sometimes it would mean a woman and her man fighting.

One thing that always puzzled me was that the prostitutes from the District would go to church and take flowers to put on the altar; they would never miss mass. Maybe they had not altogether forgot the way they were brought up. Some of the girls that worked in the District came from fine old Creole families. Lots of them never went back home again. Two to one, those who did were not accepted in their homes, as they had brought great disgrace to their families.

The District always attracted a lot of tourists, out to see all the notorious sights that they had read or heard about. And believe me, there were plenty of sights to see!

4

Chicago

In 1930 Luis Russell sent for me to come to New York and play in his band. We went to work at the Saratoga Club. Russell was one of the top bands in those days. Red Allen, Otis Johnson, and I were on trumpet; J. C. Higginbotham, trombone; Albert Nicholas, alto saxophone and clarinet; Charlie Holmes, alto sax; Greely Walton, tenor sax; Will Johnson, banjo; Pops Foster, bass; and Paul Barbarin, drums. Luis Russell himself, he played piano.

Everyone made me welcome in New York, but I didn't like it much there. Besides, I was a transfer member of Local 802, and you had to be in town a year before being accepted. So I wasn't with Luis Russell very long, only about six months, and did not make any records with this band.

While I was in New York a girl from New Orleans by the name of Hazel Prudon threw a gumbo dinner party for me and invited Jelly Roll Morton and Barney Bigard. Barney, who was also from New Orleans, was at the Cotton Club with Duke Ellington.

Jelly Roll and I went over to the Lafayette Theater after the dinner. He wanted to talk to me about making some records with him and wanted Lorenzo Tio, Jr., and me on them. I said I would, but to tell the truth, I was still mad with Jelly Roll from the time in 1924 that he took my tune "Fish Tail Blues" away from me, so

65

when the day came for the recording session I hid in my room and wouldn't make the date — and I am sorry now that I did not.

I left Luis Russell and went to Chicago to work in Dave Peyton's band at the Regal Theater. This was a good outfit, so when the Regal job ended we went out on a long tour, playing St. Louis, Kansas City, Indianapolis, Cincinnati, Columbus, Philadelphia, and the Lafayette Theater in New York. On this trip with us was Tommy Brookins, a fine dancer who was once married to Ethel Waters.

Peyton was a pianist. He had a seventeen-piece band that consisted of four trumpets, two trombones, four reeds, three violins, a guitar, a bass, drums, and a piano. But mainly it was a stage band, not a real jazz orchestra. They played a lot of overtures and things like that and didn't swing. Each man was a finished musician, but I was the only real jazz player the band had and was featured on all the solos. Peyton also had me do the vocals — the first time I ever sung in my life.

When we got to Kansas City we played a dance hall that also featured Bennie Moten's band, with Count Basie on piano. Now, of course, this was a swinging band, and I would have liked to have gone over to Moten. Peyton had not played a dance job in a long time.

While we were in Kansas City I went to see my old friend Udell Wilson. He had left New Orleans to go back home to K.C. to live, but now he missed New Orleans. Bennie Moten told me where he lived.

After the tour was over I quit Peyton's band and went back to New Orleans, but I didn't stay there very long. About 1931 a bunch of us left town to play on an excursion to Chicago. Davey Jones had the band. Everybody was having fun but me — Lillian wouldn't let me get with the bunch after we finished playing.

A funny thing happened during that trip. The white guy that gave the excursion would leave the railroad car that was set apart for white people and go back to the car where the music was so he and his girl could dance. Finally, the conductor asked the excursion promoter if he was white, telling him that if he was to go back to his own coach and stay there. But this white man said no, he was colored and belonged with us. The conductor scratched his head and stood there looking at him; he just couldn't figure it out. After that, this guy stayed back there in the car with us musicians all the time. He was a well-known fellow who always followed all the jazz musicians in New Orleans. In fact, they used to go to his place to drink; it was an after-hours joint.

Not long after we got to Chicago, Louis and Lil Armstrong had my wife and me over to dinner. Me and Louis were pretty close friends then — as we still are. I have always thought a lot of him as a person and, of course, have the greatest respect for his playing. We used to go swimming together in Lake Michigan — Louis always could swim like a fish.

I decided to stay in Chicago and be on my own, so later in 1931 I went to work at a place called King Tut's Tomb, at 47th Street and Michigan Avenue. Professor Cook, the promoter and dancer, had the show there and was also master of ceremonies, and I led the band. I had playing with me Jesse Washington, saxophone; Diamond Lil Hardaway, piano; Dan Dixon, guitar; Bill Johnson, who had been with King Oliver, bass; and Ernest Parker, drums. Of course, visiting musicians, like Louis and Lil, Johnny and Baby Dodds, and many others, would come and sit in with us too.

I did not stay at King Tut's Tomb very long. My next job was at the Chin Chow, 47th and South Parkway, and from there I went to work with Albert Ammons, the famous boogie-woogie piano player, at the Up and Down Club. We stayed there for a pretty long time until one night some guy walked in and stuck the place up. He ordered us to keep the music going while he went ahead with the holdup. You know that we played like hell, just like he said to! That was the last of that place.

Also about 1931 I had a band on North Clark Street at a spot called the Paradise Club. This was a little better for money. (Later on, this same place was known as the Victory Club, and I worked there from 1945 until into 1951, when I left to go on my first tour of Europe.)

Playing on North Clark Street so many years, I guess no musician ever got to know it any better than I did. Politicians, lawyers, doctors, musicians, pickpockets, pimps, prostitutes, and drug addicts — they all crossed paths on North Clark. There was jazz, ballads, and hillbilly music, all yours for the asking. North Clark, that was once known as "The Valley," had plenty of strip joints and clip joints, too. But it was the "gay white way" and, along with some regrets, gave me many of the happiest hours of my life. On this street I had some of the finest people in the world to beat a path to see and hear me during all those years, especially after I began at the Victory Club.

But going back to 1931 and the Paradise Club, I had George "Cockeye" Harris on piano, Elmo Allen on drums, and Rocky Casmier on saxophone. With myself on trumpet, that made up our four-piece band.

Joe Stacks, another New Orleans guy, had the intermission show there. His band made their own instruments. This was a drifters' band — the reason they went north was that a rich man from New York was in New Orleans once for Mardi Gras while they were playing on Canal Street, and he heard them. They were so good that this man took them back to New York with him when he went home. Stacks's group made good money wherever they went, and Ben Bernie wanted to use them once in an act he had. But they didn't want to appear in any high-class cabaret, as they would rather hustle on the streets or play from one joint to another.

When Joe Stacks and his buddies came to Chicago, I got them to play intermissions for me. I was blowing like everything at this time, but that didn't mean anything to those guys. The trumpet player would come in behind me and play what I played, note for note. They would also listen to Louis Armstrong's records and blow exactly the same things he did. This band was so good that the boss of the place next door to where I was playing wanted them to come to work for him. They refused, but the only reason was because they liked me. I have not seen anyone like them yet — I know that they made a fortune. They had no manager, so Professor Cook tried to be their manager, but they wanted no part of him.

I remember one night Joe Stacks came up to me and wanted to know if I needed any money; the guy had a roll of bills big enough to choke an alligator. Stacks said that if Joe Lindsay — a trombone player who was considered one of the best-dressed musicians downtown — could afford to pay thirty dollars for imported hats, then he could do even better. So Stacks sent to Italy and had a hat made for himself that he said cost one hundred dollars. I think that maybe he stretched the truth a little bit on that one, I don't know.

Before he joined Joe Stacks's outfit, Sam — that was their bazooka player — used to go around on Canal Street in New Orleans and blow on a comb with a piece of paper across it. Now, this was the only band that Lulu White would ever let into her house. I don't know yet how they did it, but they were just like One-Eye Conley — they were the world's greatest gate crashers! And I don't care what place they got into, that outfit played more jazz than any band can play today.

Things was pretty rough in Chicago during those years on account of the depression, so I went from one place to another. I was at Charlie Banner's place, at Broadway and Montrose, but did not stay there. Then I went to work for Johnny Moore; he was one of the greatest bosses that I have ever worked for, and he did me a lot of favors. I had a four-piece band there at Johnny Moore's Hi-Ho Club. With me were Bert Curry, saxophone; Joe Strater, drums;[1] and Teddy Cole, Cozy Cole's brother, piano. This was about 1932.

I also played the Harlem Nut House with Curry, Strater, and William Barbee on piano — only four pieces, but we had a big floor show. Our boss was Bon Bon Allegretti, another fine man to work for. At first Brown and Brown had the show, but later on I brought Professor Cook in with a fast revue. We made plenty of money there. One night Ralph Capone came in with his party, and we made it that time. Why, you would have thought the depression was over with right then, the way they spent money!

The next year I started playing at the Derby Club, on State Street out in Calumet City, where I worked on and off for six years. The owner was a guy called Joe Barrelhouse; his real name, though, was Regal. The band there was Edgar Saucier, alto saxophone; John Cameron, tenor sax; George Washington, also on alto; Henry Simeon, piano; and Strater, drums. On the show bill we had Billy Mitchell from the Club Delisa on the South Side of Chicago.

[1] Probably Joe Stroughter, who was mentioned in Chapter 2.

Billy had a big following, and we kept the Derby Club packed every night.

We did a lot of drinking on this job. There was a big water pitcher filled with gin on the bandstand, and everybody stayed drunk all the time. I got so that I was weighing two hundred and thirty pounds — that's the most I ever weighed in my life. The girls in the chorus used to call me "Fatty."

One night, Henry Simeon and me took two of the Derby Club hostesses out with us, but they happened to be the girlfriends of some tough hoodlums out there. Someone told these men about us going to the Club Delisa. So they questioned the girls and also beat them up. One of them finally spilled everything, the whole story. Joe Strater was waiting for Henry and me the following night when we got off the streetcar to go into the club for the night's job. Joe told us not to go in, that we would be killed if we did. I didn't even wait around for the next streetcar to come along; I walked all the way back to Chicago.

I hated to give up that job, though, because we were making such good money, so the next night I went back and asked for Joe Barrelhouse, but he wasn't there. In the meantime, everybody was looking at me like I had committed some kind of terrible crime. I went to the bar to get a drink, and someone asked if I thought I was going to work. And then I noticed that a new band had come in and was setting up.

I was good and drunk by the time that Joe came in. He said I wasn't working there anymore, but I told him that it was a mistake, that the girls had lied. Now, he knew perfectly well it was me that was lying, but Joe liked me, so finally he said I should go back to work but never let anything like that happen again.

I went over to the bandstand and ordered the new band to get off, but they said that the boss had given them my job. So then I told them that I was the boss and that my band was going on that night as usual. Meanwhile, Joe was standing at the bar killing himself laughing. I brought in another show and fired the dancer that told the boss about Henry and me taking the two hostesses out. Joe liked Henry Simeon, too, and wanted him to come back to work, but he wouldn't at that time. Henry did come back in later years, though.

70

Lee with a younger brother, probably John, about 1906. *(Courtesy Mary Collins)*

Fourteen-year-old Lee after being turned away from playing at the Tuxedo Dance Hall. *(Courtesy Mary Collins)*

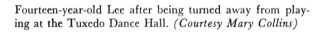

Lee in 1923, shortly before joining Joe Oliver's band in Chicago. *(Courtesy Mary Collins)*

Lee's band in Dallas, 1925 or 1926. From the left: Coke Eye Bob (Arthur Joseph?), Mary Brown, Freddie "Boo-Boo" Miller, Octave Crosby, Henry Julien, "Professor" Sherman Cook, Lee, and Percy Darensburg. *(Courtesy Danny Barker)*

The Entertainers Club on Franklin Street in New Orleans (1942), where Lee played in 1925 and 1926. *(Photograph by Bill Russell)*

The Astoria Hotel, New Orleans (1942), where the Jones-Collins Astoria Hot Eight played. *(Photograph by Bill Russell)*

Italian Hall (Union Italiana), New Orleans (1961), where the Jones-Collins Astoria Hot Eight recordings were made. *(Photograph by Bill Russell)*

Lee while playing at the Ship in Chicago about 1940. *(Courtesy Mary Collins)*

Chicago was a great jazz town even during the depression. Rocco Gallo's Club 29, at 47th and Dearborn, was a good spot where musicians went to sit in. Johnny and Baby Dodds worked there, with Natty Dominique on trumpet. One night Louis and Lil Armstrong came in, and they seemed so loving and happy that everyone thought, or hoped, that they were going back together again. Louis had just got back from a successful European tour, so this must have been in 1935.

Another place in Chicago where you could hear some fine music during these times was at the H & T. When you walked in there you would see a guy playing a kazoo and another guy playing on some drums. The drummer was none other than my old friend Snags, and the kazoo player was Mr. Tampa Red (Hudson Whittaker), one of the early blues singers and guitar players to make records. They were so fine that you would really have thought that there were more than two guys playing. The pair of them kept the H & T crowded, and on my nights off I used to go there to play along. Now, you really had to play some in a honky-tonk place like that in order to satisfy the type of customers they had.

One day while I was rehearsing for a recording date I started blowing some lowdown blues, and Tampa Red got in there with me on his guitar and kazoo. Between only the two of us we sounded like a three-piece band. I don't know what happened to Tampa Red; he just finally passed out of the picture, I guess.

Another job I remember real well was with a band that Zutty Singleton had at the Three Deuces, on State and Lake streets. In this combination was myself on trumpet — I replaced Vernell York — Scoops Carey, alto saxophone; Milton Hinton, bass; Everett Barksdale, guitar; Teddy Cole, piano; and Zutty, drums. Zinky Cohn was the pianist before Teddy came in, and Art Tatum played intermission piano. Roy Eldridge joined the band later and became leader.

I made some recordings with blues singers in 1935 and 1936 that gave me a lot of pleasure. One session was with Richard M. Jones, a fine pianist and composer from New Orleans. Just the two of us made "Trouble in Mind" and "Black Rider," which was issued on Bluebird Records. I believe they were the only blues vocals Jones ever recorded.

Then I accompanied Lil Johnson, who made many fine blues records during the thirties. We had J. H. "Freddie" Shayne on piano and a guitar player and a drummer whose names I forget. Also in 1936 I made some recordings with Victoria Spivey. She was a famous blues singer in New York in the early twenties, and she recorded for many years. In the band accompanying her we had myself on trumpet, Freddie Shayne at the piano, and John Lindsay on bass, and I think Arnett Nelson was on clarinet.

I stayed out to Calumet City for a number of years, until November, 1939. I liked Joe Barrelhouse very much; he was very good to me. My two-year-old daughter, Lillian, died in 1936 while I was at the Derby Club, and Joe Barrelhouse told me not to worry about funeral expenses, that he would take care of everything. That went to my heart. Not only that, but so many other nice things he did for me.

After I closed at the Derby Club I took to hanging out in a tough, third-rate Chicago cabaret called the All Star. This place was at 43rd Street and Indiana Avenue. The blues singer who was there then was Lil Green, a great gal that you don't hear any more talk about these days. She had Edgar Saucier with her on saxophone, Jack Cooley on drums, and a piano player named Charlie, who was from New Orleans. They sounded so good that I would go home to get my trumpet and sit in with them. I was playing along about an hour one night when the boss asked me where was I working. I told him I had just quit out at Calumet City but wasn't doing anything much just then, so he asked me to go to work for him. I said I would if I didn't have anything else to do. That happened to be the night that "In the Dark," a song which became very popular, was born.

The All Star was always packed with musicians, as a lot of them were out of work. Some had never heard of me before, so they would come in every night to listen to Lil Green sing and me play trumpet.

Lil was one of the greatest singers, but she died in 1954 at the height of her career. She was very famous while she was alive, though, and played theater dates in all the major cities. Besides singing, Lil composed a lot of songs; one of them was "Why Don't You Do Right?" I was supposed to record with her once, but did not, due to money matters. I still hate it that the record deal with Lil didn't work out.

During these years there was also a blues singer by the name of Doctor Clayton out of Vicksburg, Mississippi. He was very popular and made a lot of records. "Danny Boy" was his favorite, and he could really sing it, but he was more of a blues singer. A lot of mornings he would tell me that he was going out to Melrose Music and get some money that he said Melrose owed him for recordings. Doctor Clayton was a heavy drinker and never made too much money even though he made quite a few records and the jukeboxes all over town were playing them. I think that he died around 1946.

Times was pretty tough after I left Calumet City, but I finally managed to land a steady job at the Ship, located on North Clark Street near Ontario. At one time or another I was also manager, bouncer, and master of ceremonies there, besides leading the band and playing trumpet. I started working at the Ship in 1940 — and that came about more or less by accident one Saturday night when I was out scouting for a job with Theodore "Bucket" Crosby, my drummer, and a piano player named William Flakes. (Bucket wasn't a soloist like a lot of drummers are today; he was a band drummer that could make you play like hell. The first time I ever saw him was years before when he was working on the riverboats with Fate Marable and Red Allen.) Bucket and Flakes and me walked up North Clark and came to a place — this was the Ship — that had a canopy stretched across the sidewalk out to the street. The door of this place was never locked. There was a woman looking out the door. She called us in and asked us to play something for her. In fact, she wanted us to play there as a job. I asked her what she was paying, but she said we'd have to wait about that until the boss came in.

Work was slow; we didn't mind waiting, but we figured we might as well be playing something in the meantime. We made twenty dollars apiece in tips. So when the boss finally got there about seven o'clock the next morning, which was Sunday, I told him we'd like to work there regular. But I also wanted to know what he was paying, and he told us that he would not pay more than one dollar a night. I argued with him, but that didn't do any good; he stuck to that one dollar. I talked it over with my boys, and they decided to stay with me.

To add insult to that one dollar business, the boss decided he'd put on a floor show, too. To see the women he wanted us to play for, you'd have thought that the customers would get up and walk out of the place. The youngest one was about forty years old; this was a real shocker! Believe it or not, though, the place was packed every night with people watching these women prancing around the floor in a sort of half strip tease. Out of this bunch there was only one, Patsy, that was better looking and could sing. She was all the show herself, just a singer — and a pretty good one at that.

I asked the manager one night if he would change the floor show, as we were getting tired of those old women. I told Patsy to put in a good show and get some good dancers. The boss went along with us on this, so we did get a pretty fair show. We had a dancer called Snake Hips (not the original entertainer by that name, though) and his wife to take over the floor show.

The doorman at the Ship was a quaint character from New Orleans — we called him Cry Baby because he had kind of a funny sob to his voice. But he was a hustler; he would stand out front on the sidewalk and yell out to passing cars and pedestrians, "Never a dull moment, floor show going on inside right now. We've got Lee Collins, New Orleans trumpet player — best in the city, folks." Sometimes we'd be on our intermission when Cry Baby would rush in with a bunch of customers in tow. He'd sing out, "Lee, hit a note for these people." One thing about Cry Baby, when he brought a party in they would usually turn out to be good spenders. And he was sure to get his tip, too.

We were still making that one dollar per night in wages, but that didn't worry us any. I always had money in my pockets and plenty of clothes; anyone would have thought that we were making no less than one hundred and fifty dollars a week. But our money was all tips. Anyway, I was not crying the blues like a lot of musicians I knew — some of them had to go to work on the WPA. There was always plenty of show people and musicians to visit me during intermissions, and I sure gave away a lot of liquor. It didn't cost me anything.

A funny thing was that the manager took after me and began

to buy me all kinds of beautiful shirts and ties. This woman wasn't worrying none about the money she spent, as she had charge of the place, including the cash register. But I had eyes for no one at that time; I had money on my mind. Then too, I was happy at home. But as time went along, the manager and I did sort of make up, and she got so jealous that I couldn't hardly talk to the girls. One of the girls asked me one night to play a special song for her. She gave me a pretty-good-sized tip, saying that she was blue for her boyfriend. Kitty, the crazy woman that was the manager, saw the money change hands, so she slapped the poor girl in the face. Then Kitty had the girl — who, of course, did not know what the fuss was all about — barred from the place.

For a bouncer we had a large Polish woman that we called Big Lil; she was about six feet tall and weighed maybe two hundred pounds. Big Lil was just as good as any man for the job of bouncer; you could depend on her to bounce anyone that got out of line. I was weighing about two hundred and fifteen at the time, so I was a pretty fair bouncer myself.

There were a lot of hostesses at this place — B-girls, you would call them — that made as much as a hundred dollars a night. They thought themselves above prostitutes, as they never went out with a man. What they did was to give a customer a big buildup so as to make him keep on spending his money. Then, after his money was all gone, he would get an equally big letdown. Many a night we had to pull some poor sap off one of those girls. You could spot a B-girl if you watched close enough, because some of them had a habit of tearing matchbook covers in strips; that was the way they kept tabs on their drinks.

I remember a fellow that came in one night and spent quite a large sum of money. All you could hear in the place was that a "big hat" man — meaning a guy with plenty of money — blew into town. One of the B-girls was helping to relieve him of that big bankroll he had on him by sending drinks up to the bandstand and, in fact, buying drinks for everybody. Even so, his money didn't seem to run out. After he had spent maybe three or four hundred dollars, he demanded this girl to leave with him, but she slipped out through the back door. All hell busted loose when he discovered that the B-girl had run out on him; all the bartenders, bouncers, and porters put together couldn't hold him down. The last thing the management wanted was to call the police, but that is what they finally had to do. Even the police had to call for reinforcements. But the place was about wrecked by that time.

One nice thing about the Ship, we were all just like one big, happy family. On Christmas Eve we would have a big tree in the place, and everybody exchanged presents. And we were doing all right financially, too. The master of ceremonies and his wife bought a new car and had money in the bank, and the girls in the show were all buying themselves fur coats. No one had any money worries except the manager, and that was only because the boss finally caught up with her stealing. So she lost her job, and all the bartenders got fired, also. In a way, I couldn't feel sorry for Kitty. As a matter of fact, she had begun to get on my nerves to the point where many a night I felt like I wanted to quit. Even after this woman got fired, though, she would still come around and chin with the chorus girls. This got to be very annoying after a while.

A lot of my fans would ask me why I kept on working on North Clark Street. I told them that I had been with big bands and that sometimes I had the bad luck to be stranded somewhere and would have to send for money so as to get back home. I had a family to provide for, so there was not any point in chasing all over the country without making any money, sometimes not even meeting my expenses. At least I was making money on North Clark and not living under a financial strain all the time.

I was looking out the window one night and noticed a little woman pass the Ship. I could not see her face, but I thought I knew her from her walk. So I ran outside and called to her. Just as I thought, it was little Mary Spriggs. Little Mary — everyone called her that because she was so small — and me had been friends for a long time but hadn't seen each other in quite a while. We used to meet often when I would go to Louis Armstrong's home or visit Barney Bigard on his trips to Chicago with Ellington. They were all her friends, too. As I say, I hadn't seen her recently, but I knew that Mary had her mother and daughter with her and was taking care of them. And I had read in the newspapers about her sister's death not too long before.

Mary was some surprised to see me. She said she had quit

her job out at the Club Delisa and was down on North Clark to see about a new job. I invited her in for a drink and introduced her to the band and also to the different girls. I felt sorry for her and wanted to help if I could, so I asked Mary if she would care to work at the Ship. She said yes, but opened her eyes wide and changed her mind when I told her what we were getting paid. Then I explained about how we made all those good tips and said that she could make it there too. Mary liked the Ship very much, once she began working there. Sometimes we wouldn't leave the place until late in the morning.

The dressing room was in back of the bar, and someone had cut a hole through to the place where the liquor was stored. It was in big gallon jugs, so there was never any problem about getting enough to drink. One morning Elmo Allen, the drummer, invited us all to his home, saying that he had plenty to drink, so we took a cab over to his place. When we got there, he had two gallons of whiskey — of course, I knew right away where it came from — but we didn't worry about that any. Everybody in the entire show got drunk. When I got to work the next night, the boss told me we should have drunk something better — that way we could have been to work on time. He laughed like everything at us, but he didn't say any more about it because he knew he was not paying us anything to speak of.

I fired Elmo Allen one Sunday morning in a fit of anger. Thinking it over later, I decided to go and hire him back. Elmo lived just across the street from Mary, so after I got him to promise me that he would come back to work I decided I might as well go over and visit Mary, since I was so close to her place anyway. Elmo wanted to come along, but I knew that Mary was funny about anyone coming to see her so early. I didn't even know how she would accept me, let alone Elmo, so I told him that he could not go.

Mary was surprised to see me at the door, but she invited me in and introduced me to the landlady and the landlady's boyfriend, explaining that we had been friends a long time. I spent the day there, talking and drinking. Later that evening I got tired, so I asked Mary if I could lie down in her room awhile. She said yes, to go ahead, that she was going out to see her mother and daughter.

I didn't much care if I went home or not because Lillian and I were not getting along so good at this time. Mary called about eight o'clock to tell me to get up and come have dinner with her, as it was almost time to go to work. Mary's landlady began to tease her about me; she told her, "I thought that you told me you two are only friends." Mary laughed and said it was true, that we were friends.

Now, Mary had mentioned a boyfriend of hers to me. He was out of the city just then but was expected back soon. One night she brought him to the Ship with her when she came to work. He seemed like a nice person, but I could tell right away that Mary did not act as though she was in love with him. Mary kept on watching every move I made, and then it came to me that I was in love with her. So I asked her how serious she was with this other man. Mary said it was nothing much, just someone to keep company with. We had a long talk, and I ended up asking her if she thought that we could make it together. Mary said we could try.

I had attempted several times to patch things up with Lillian, but it just didn't work out, and so we got divorced in 1950. Mary and I were married later in Indiana. I want to make it clear that Mary had nothing to do with Lillian and me breaking up; we had already separated before I started going with Mary. In fact, Mary and Lillian got to be good friends, and there was no bad feelings between them.

Now, as I have said before, I always seemed to run in the luck of jealous girlfriends. I was sitting at a table one night, flirting with a girl that played piano at a place down the street. At one time, before Mary and I started, I used to take her to the breakfast dances out at the Club Delisa. While we were talking, the girl noticed Mary watching us, so she asked if Mary and I were anything to each other, and I said no. Because if we were, she said, she was going to leave, as she had had some kind of trouble with Mary once years before and did not want any more of it. She said Mary could cause plenty of trouble. I knew that Mary had a lot of temper, but I didn't think she would say anything there at the Ship. Just then, Mary walked up to us and asked if it wasn't time for me to go on the bandstand. This girl just flew out of the place, and Mary and me let the whole business drop.

But it looked like the devil was always busy! Kitty, the woman who had got fired as manager of the Ship, came in one night and sat down at a table with a girl that we called Big Helen. When Mary arrived, she went over to the table where Big Helen and Kitty were sitting. I was on the bandstand playing, afraid to even look in their direction. All that I could see was a table going over and Kitty shaking her head while Mary talked to her. Big Helen said later that Mary told Kitty to stay away from the Ship if she didn't want trouble — that she was going with Lee Collins now. Big Helen always said that little Mary was not afraid of anything.

I always was a sucker for trying to help New Orleans musicians. A young man came into the Ship one time and told me he was Joe White, a drummer from New Orleans. I believed him and gave him a job — he kind of reminded me of a snare drummer by the same name out of Jackson, Mississippi. (This Joe White — the one from Jackson, I mean — was the world's greatest! A funny thing is that no one has ever thought to mention him in a book. But maybe the reason they didn't is that he always followed the minstrel shows.) Anyway, Mary found out later that the Joe White who I had hired was not from New Orleans at all. She asked him about some place down there that he couldn't have helped but know about if he was really from our home town. Like Mary said, he should have known at least something about New Orleans if he was born there like he claimed, so I asked him point blank to tell me the truth. He said the reason he lied was that someone told him he was sure to land a job with me if he let on he was from New Orleans — that I was known to always hire New Orleans musicians first.

Mary was always encouraging me to be on the lookout for something better than the Ship. She'd say, "Lee, you know you're too good a trumpet player to stay here. These honky-tonks are all right for a while, but keep on looking for something better." I told her she knew my reasons and that we would leave when times got better, but in the meantime, the Ship was the only place I had found where I could make a decent living. I had two boys to bring up and educate, and I didn't want them to suffer for anything. (Lee, Jr., was born December 23, 1931, and Earl on November 21,

1933. I also had another son, Leeds, who was born in 1924, but he died two years later.)

Good things don't last always. We lost Cry Baby, our doorman, when he went to a different job. So the boss asked me if I could get another one, but the man I hired turned out to be a wrong guy. He cut a man and almost got the place closed up.

Later on, I moved further down on North Clark to a place that was called the Firehouse. The combination I had there was Jeep Robinson on tenor saxophone, Eurreal "Little Brother" Montgomery on piano, and Jimmy Bertrand, a great little Creole fellow and musician who had migrated from Biloxi to Chicago, on drums. Jimmy also played xylophone. He had been with Erskine Tate's orchestra at the Vendome Theater along with Armstrong and Teddy Weatherford, a fine pianist that later went to China and India and died over there in 1945. Jimmy was supposed to go to Europe once with Eddie South, the violinist, but he got drunk and missed the boat. Another time, I hired him to come to work with me, but he never showed up until five days later — and then he wasn't able to do anything. Jimmy could play symphony music as well as jazz, and he was the teacher of Big Sidney Catlett and a lot of other Chicago drummers who also turned out to be great. But Jimmy Bertrand's trouble was whiskey and women — both have turned many a musician into a has-been.

All this time I was looking for another place to work, like Mary wanted me to, so I went out to South Chicago to a place called Louie's. This place was in a basement, and there was a poolroom and gambling tables in the rear. Louie was a great talker; he claimed that he was once one of the best pool sharks around. He said he played the famous Pensacola Kid. Jelly Roll Morton told me that he had played the Pensacola Kid, too, but I never was a pool player, so I don't know any more about him.

I only had three pieces at Louie's and was anxious to get Mary out there with me, so I told Louie I had a girl drummer and wanted her to be in the band. Louie agreed to that. I knew that Mary could hold up with my help, because the most we had at Louie's was polkas, and we would not play anything too hard for her. World War II was coming on, and everybody began making money. Louie wanted us to stay at his place, but I had no intention of doing so.

Someone told me about a club on Commercial Avenue, and, sure enough, I was hired, but Mary couldn't go there as a drummer, so she went to work as a barmaid down in Spring Valley, about six miles from La Salle, Illinois. She telephoned me one night to see if I wanted to take a job at a place called Tenny's at La Salle. That meant I could be near her, so I told her I would. Mary made all the arrangements, and I wired to New Orleans for musicians. I couldn't get the ones I wanted, but I did hire some that were highly recommended.

Now, Tenny's was a fine place; the people were wonderful to work for, the pay was tops, and they booked all the big acts. There was all kinds of gambling; the only trouble was that some of the boys liked to gamble too much. We had two very good old-time comedians on the show bill who stayed at the dice table all the time that they weren't working. Some pay nights they would have no pay coming to them at all on account of gambling. I made a try at the dice once and almost lost all my money. Mary gave me the devil, saying she thought I was smart enough to know I couldn't beat the house.

I ran into Red Allen in Chicago one night I had off from my job at Tenny's, so he and I rode around awhile in his car and then I decided to call Mary. Her boss answered the telephone and told me that Mary was in the hospital. I couldn't speak for a moment; I knew that she had been all right when I left her. I went around to Mary's daughter's place and told her about it, but I didn't want to tell her mother because she was easy to get upset and was not over the shock yet of losing her other daughter. Antoinette, Mary's daughter, and I caught a bus for La Salle. When we got to the hospital, Mary had a big smile on her face, and I knew that she was all right. She had had the presence of mind to call a doctor when she first got sick, and he ordered her to the hospital right away for an emergency appendectomy. It was a lucky thing her appendix did not burst.

Mary's mother was so worried when she found out what had happened that we came back to Chicago. I then went to work at the Casa Blanca on North Clark Street. This was 1941–42; the war was on for real now, and people had plenty of money to spend. This band had Little Brother Montgomery on piano, a white clarinet player from Detroit (I can't recall his name now), and a very nice Japanese kid called Joe on drums. Joe went for Chinese, though, because everyone was down on the Japanese because of the war. The Casa Blanca was a small place, so our four-piece band was just right for it. We decided to stay there as long as we made plenty of money.

I remember one night a squad car rolled up in front of the Casa Blanca and a couple of cops came in and asked me if I was Lee Collins. When I said yes, I was, they told me to get my horn and come with them outside to their car. As we were getting in the policemen asked me if I knew Paul Mares — he was the famous white cornet player that led the New Orleans Rhythm Kings back in the 1920's. I did know him, of course, and it turned out that Paul was opening a place of his own and wanted me there. When I got there I found Baby Dodds, Georg Brunis, Muggsy Spanier, and some of the guys out of Bob Crosby's band all sitting on the bandstand. Paul was acting as bartender and blowing horn at the same time. From ten o'clock that night until eight the next morning we played all the great New Orleans standards. But my boss was some angry with me when I went to work the next night.

There were some young hoodlums that used to hang out at the Casa Blanca. One night I noticed them whispering to each other, and I began to wonder what was going to happen. Then I saw one of them talking to Mary. So when I got a chance, I asked her what was the trouble. She said they told her that the police were coming, and then one of the hoods gave her his gun, asking Mary to hide it for him in her big purse. He was afraid that he would be searched — and this was known as a tough police squad. I told Mary never to do anything like that again.

The funny part is that all but one of those guys are dead now, and the one exception is a fine businessman today — I used to like him because you could see that he didn't really belong with that gang. I would talk to him a lot, telling him to quit running around with those hoodlums.

In 1941 I went into a hospital with pneumonia. That was a hard blow, because I had never been sick a day in my life. I was told I would have to stay in bed for quite a while and then rest up for a few more weeks. But instead of following the doctor's orders, I went back to work in a week. Old man pneumonia had taken his toll, though, for I began to wheeze and have shortness of breath. So I went to see the doctor again, and he diagnosed my trouble as asthma. I didn't believe him, as I could still blow my trumpet like I always had, but I soon found out that the doctor was right and I was wrong.

Many a night I would have to take off from the job and go to the hospital to get a shot so that I could catch my breath. Finally, the doctor told me to quit playing awhile. I got to wondering what else in the world I could do if the time ever came that I had to stop blowing altogether, because music was the only thing I knew. I had held a horn in my hands since I was seven years old. Music was my whole life, and I always said that the day I put my horn down and was not able to play any more, that would be the day I wanted to die. I believe now that the pneumonia and then the asthma was the first start of my long sickness; I played long and hard all those years on North Clark Street.

As luck would have it, the Casa Blanca had to close in 1945 due to a killing in the place. So I left there and went to the Victory Club — the place of all places — at 664 North Clark Street, near Erie. The boss was a great guy named Werlie Catanese. Now, the Victory Club was one of the most notorious spots on the near North Side. All kinds of people went there — from college and university students and professional people that loved jazz to such characters as Louise the Wig and Cripple Jack, a hillbilly who was known as one of the best "dips" (pickpockets) to ever come out of the South, and Indian Marie, a notorious lesbian. She used to come in, get drunk, and then start beating up on her girlfriends.

And there was One-Eye Sal, who was there every night. She would go through the same routine each time: walk up to the bandstand, hand me a dollar bill, and strut away. She did this every night. Regardless of how drunk she would be, anything we played for her was all right; she never knew the difference anyway. The musicians got so that they started calling One-Eye Sal "Mrs. Collins." The first time Mary heard them say that she looked real funny until I told her who "Mrs. Collins" was and explained what the joke was all about.

We got mostly truck drivers and barflies for customers when I first went to the Victory Club, but then pretty soon, after word got around where I was, the place would be packed and jammed every night. Most nights, in fact, you wouldn't even be able to get in at all, on account of the crowd of kids from Northwestern University and the University of Chicago. We had a lot of Indians that used to frequent the place, too; after they got drunk the show was really on! But no one was ever hurt seriously.

I drew people from the Chicago Gold Coast and universities all over the country. And jazz fans from all parts of the world would make their way to the Victory Club to hear me play.

The important thing was that I had an understanding with the boss that all the students that came there were to be protected from the rough element and treated with the utmost respect. It is the truth that no one ever dared to bother those students; they knew better, and my boss and I saw to it that the policy was carried out at all times.

I used to get a big kick out of the young people going from one night club to another but always coming back to the Victory Club before the night was over. They'd say, "Lee, we just had to come by to hear you before we go home." They said it didn't cost too much for them to come to the Victory Club, and, besides the music, they got treated to a good show just by looking at all the different characters that hung out there. I never got tired of blowing for the university students and would always play any request numbers they asked for.

I guess that my horn and me made the Victory Club's name famous all over the world. A lot of European people came there expecting to see a fine cabaret, but if they were disappointed in that way I made it up to them with the good old New Orleans jazz. As I say, I got as much kick playing for all those fine people as they did listening to me.

Every night I would get the same old questions about why was I playing on North Clark Street. A lot of musicians and fans couldn't understand this, but I was a person that didn't like to do a lot of traveling. Besides, I was making good money at the Victory

Club. Werlie gave me a raise every time I even began to think about leaving. He knew that I made his place famous, that if I was not there it would have been just another gin joint. That is also one reason why I could come and go as I pleased.

I used to take all kinds of characters that played music into my Victory Club band. One of them was Pork Chops Smith. He came from Africa and was a good drummer — when he felt like playing. Pork Chops would come to work with tears in his eyes and some wild tale about how his grandmother had died and how he needed money to go to her funeral. Werlie would ask him how much he needed, and Pork Chops would say, "Oh, about a hundred dollars." As well as Werlie knew Pork Chops, he'd let him have the money. Werlie would come to me a few weeks later and say, "Lee, where is that drummer? He's never come back yet."

Werlie was riding down the street one night and caught sight of Pork Chops. He brought him back to the club and told Pork Chops to either go back to work and pay off the money he owed or else he'd shoot him. But Pork Chops just gave Werlie some other kind of sob story and went on back down the street.

I also had Clarence Breckenridge, one of the best boogie-woogie piano players in Chicago. He would sit at the piano with a cigarette dangling from the corner of his mouth while he was playing. Will Leonard put an article about Clarence and a picture of him in the *Chicago Tribune*.

Some of the other musicians that worked for me at the Victory Club at one time or another were Charlie Davis, Chink Hester, Little Brother Montgomery, Frank "Sweets" Williams, and Bill Thompson, piano; Charles Stewart, Jeep Robinson, and Edgar Saucier, tenor saxophone; Oliver Alcorn and Arnett Nelson, clarinet; Anderson Saucier, Freddie Flynn, Buzz Hayes, and Carl Williams, drums; and Charlie McBride, vocal.

Once when I was at the Victory Club I decided to quit drinking hard liquor for a while; I had it in my mind to drink champagne, thinking that wouldn't hurt me. So I went on a champagne kick, but anyone who drinks that knows the results afterwards. One night I had too much and fell asleep at a table. While I was sleeping, a dope addict, of all people, took my watch and money off of me. I didn't say anything to anyone when I woke up — I felt very foolish, as I had always been against my musicians getting drunk. But the next night this addict — it happened to be a girl — came in and said, "Lee, I couldn't do you any harm because you're a very nice guy. So here is your watch and money back." I was the most surprised man you would ever want to see — I had not expected to get my things back again.

I made some recordings with Bertha "Chippie" Hill, the old-time blues singer (she would turn over in her grave if she knew I called her "old-time"), in Chicago in February, 1946, for Rudi Blesh's Circle Records. The tunes we recorded were "Trouble in Mind," "Careless Love," "Charleston Blues," "How Long Blues," "Around the Clock Blues," and "Nobody Knows You When You're Down and Out." Chippie really moaned the blues on "Trouble in Mind." Accompanying Chippie was myself on trumpet; Lovie Austin, piano (Freddie Shayne also played piano on a couple of the tunes); John Lindsay, bass; and Baby Dodds, drums.

The Hot Club of Chicago, which was directed by Catherine Jacobson, John Schenck, and George Hoefer, gave a lot of jazz concerts at the Moose Hall on North Dearborn Street. The Hot Club was the one that had Bunk Johnson come to Chicago for a concert at Orchestra Hall in September, 1946. The only thing I was sorry about was that Bunk was brought back when he was old; I'd seen him great, and I hated to see him pitiful like he was that night. The thing was, the train he came up from New Orleans on was late arriving the night of the concert, and so he had no time to rest up before playing. His lip was not in good shape at all. But, still and all, he was Bunk, and that was what the people wanted to see. With him on the concert bill was Preston Jackson, trombone; Darnell Howard, clarinet; Snags Jones, drums; John Lindsay, bass; Don Ewell, piano; Lonnie Johnson, guitar; myself on trumpet; the Jimmy Yancey trio; and, for a special feature, Baby Dodds on solo drums.

Later on, I also played another concert with Bunk in Chicago. The other musicians that time included Jimmy McPartland, trumpet; Edmond Hall, clarinet; Don Ewell and Jimmy Yancey, pianos; Freddie Flynn, drums; Big Bill Broonzy, blues singer; and a trombonist whose name I have forgotten.

86

Sometimes Bunk would drop in at the Victory Club. He used to tell Werlie about the big contracts he had and how he was expecting to get a thousand dollars soon. When he was broke, though, and needed money for drinks, he'd tell the boss to hold his diamond (zircon) ring. But Werlie just laughed and said, "Keep your ring, Pops, and buy what you need."

Early in 1947 I recorded "Swingin' with Lee" (my own composition), "El Ritmo" (another one of my tunes), "Long Time Ago," and "Woman That I Love" with Little Brother Montgomery's quintet. In the band, besides Little Brother Montgomery on piano and myself on trumpet, was Oliver Alcorn, clarinet and tenor sax; Ernie Crawford, bass; and Pork Chops Smith, drums. The recordings were made by Robert Stendahl and came out on the Century label.

In 1948 I went to New York with Kid Ory to play a concert at Carnegie Hall and another one in Rhode Island. They were both promoted by John Schenck, a wonderful guy. The band included Kid Ory and me, Joe Darensbourg on clarinet, Ed Garland on bass, Ram Hall on drums, and Little Brother Montgomery on piano. We had a lot of fun on this trip, and everyone was in good spirits. Little Brother liked to drink, and so did John Schenck; after the liquor ran out one night at the hotel, John was down to drinking bay rum. That was the night I found Little Brother out in the hall sitting in front of the three elevators, just staring at them. I asked him what was wrong, and he said nothing was wrong, he was just looking at the people riding up and down on the elevators. I knew he was drunk, so I finally got him to bed.

We played a concert at Orchestra Hall after coming back to Chicago, and then Ory went home to Los Angeles. About a month later I received a letter from him wanting me to go out there. I wanted to, but my expenses were very high, and the money he offered me wasn't enough to take care of them. You see, I was paying Lillian a large sum of money to keep her quiet. Then, too, if I went I wanted Mary to go with me, but she had her mother to look after. I had got used to having Mary go with me every place I went; she took care of all my business affairs and I relied on her a great deal. But I regret to this day that I did not go with Ory, because jazz had begun to decline in Chicago.

I left the Victory Club for a while in 1949 because Johnny Lane, a clarinet player, was at the Sky Club and asked me to join his band there. He also had Georg Brunis with him. I stayed there for some time, but the place was too far for me to travel, so I went back to the Victory Club.

But I took off again in 1950 to go with a very good five-piece band that the pianist Art Hodes took into Frank Holzfeind's Blue Note. We had Zutty Singleton on drums, Georg Brunis on trombone, and Pee Wee Russell on clarinet. We stayed there fifteen weeks, playing to a packed house every night. Besides the band, the Blue Note bill featured Chippie Hill. We all liked Chippie, but she sure did give us a rough time!

Sarah Vaughan came to the Blue Note while we were there. One night after finishing her song, Chippie stumbled on the way down from the bandstand, and Sarah went over to help her. Well, did Chippie do some cursing! One thing she told Sarah was that she wasn't too old to get off the bandstand by herself, and she did not need any damn help. I wanted to laugh but didn't dare to because I would have got the worst cursing out that you ever heard. I didn't feel like listening to Chippie call me all kinds of bad names.

Sarah had a private dressing room, as all the stars do. Chippie didn't have one, though, so she used to go in Sarah's dressing room to change. One night Sarah's manager ordered Chippie to stay out of there. That made her mad. Frank Holzfeind finally had a dressing room fixed up for Chippie in order to keep peace.

On our closing night at the Blue Note, Zutty and I took Chippie to the Club Delisa, where she had worked years before. Zutty was about to go into the band at Ruth and Bill Reinhardt's Jazz Limited, and I was going to work at the Bee Hive. On our way out we tried to talk Chippie into staying in Chicago. Zutty and I both liked Chippie and, for some reason or other, felt as if we ought to look after her, even though she had been around a long, long time. But she was determined to go back to New York, and there was no way of stopping her. When we got to the Club Delisa, Chippie hurried on ahead of us. Just as she got to the middle of the street a cab struck her and knocked her down. Zutty and I ran over to where she was and picked her up. Instead of telling us how bad she was hurt, she was giving the cab driver hell for getting her coat dirty, saying that she had just got it out of the cleaners. We thought that she was hurt, so we took her to a doctor. The poor cab driver was scared to death; Zutty and I were both big men, and I guess he figured we were detectives.

Chippie did go back to New York. Not long after that, in May, 1950, she was killed by a cab as she crossed a street. It seemed like Chippie had her warning that time in Chicago, and, as fate would have it, she was destined to die that way.

After the Blue Note engagement, I went to the Bee Hive with Miff Mole's band. I must say that Miff has to be counted as one of the greatest jazz trombonists among white musicians — and I don't leave out Brunis, either. Besides Miff and me, the Bee Hive band had Darnell Howard on clarinet, Don Ewell at piano, and Baby Dodds on drums. We carried a great crowd there; the place was too small to accommodate all the people that wanted to hear us. I asked for more money, but the boss said he couldn't see where he could pay more. I knew it wasn't that business was bad, so I finally went back to the Victory Club.

On my nights off I would go to the Mellow Inn out on the South Side and sit in with the musicians there. We had some great jam sessions. One night when Mary was there I stuck a big cigar in my mouth just to have some fun with her — she knew I didn't smoke. She got a big kick out of my cutting up. Now, I saw a woman come into the place in the meantime, but she was hiding her face and I didn't pay much attention. Just as I got off the bandstand to go over to where Mary was sitting, up jumped the devil! The woman that had come in was Lillian. She ran up to me, started tearing my clothes, and then tried to get at Mary, but I wasn't going to let her do that.

Mary just stood there looking on while the bouncer and I finally got Lillian quieted down. I told Lillian that Mary was working there and that she mustn't come in and cause trouble. Before she left, Lillian said that someone — I don't know who it was — had telephoned her to say that she could find me and my girlfriend at the Mellow Inn.

Besides the jazz concerts I already mentioned, I remember another one I did in June, 1951. This was at the Grand Theatre in Oshkosh, Wisconsin. The band I took there was Art Hodes, piano; George Winn, trombone; Jimmy Granato, clarinet; and Booker T. Washington, drums. Along with our band there were also some very good Wisconsin musicians, including Bob Anderson and Dick Ruedebusch, both trumpet players. After the concert we all went on to one of the local bars and jammed awhile.

All the time that I was at the Victory Club I kept getting letters from Europe and was expecting to go there some time for a tour. That brings to mind an article Pat Harris put in *Down Beat* magazine in July, 1949. "It is our prediction," Pat wrote, "that trumpeter Lee Collins will stay at the Victory forever, despite his perennially proposed jaunts everywhere from Siam to Alaska, none of which seem to ever work out." Pat also mentioned "the counter-show" that was always being staged by some of the customers.

Werlie, the boss, opened up a new place once that was called the Starlight Room, downstairs from the Blackstone Hotel. I took my band in there, but right away I saw that I wasn't going to get along with the manager; he didn't like anything but rhumba bands. So pretty soon we went back to the Victory Club. But no matter where I was playing, the Victory Club or any other place, I always gave my best at all times when there was real jazz fans that listened and understood what we played.

At the Twin Terrace Cafe, Chicago, March 23, 1947. From the left: Little Brother Montgomery, Lonnie Johnson, Bill Johnson, Oliver Alcorn, Jerome "Pork Chops" Smith, Lee, and Preston Jackson. *(Courtesy Jim Gordon)*

Paul "Doc" Evans, Lee, Jimmy McPartland, and Bunk Johnson at the Twin Terrace Cafe, June 29, 1947. *(Courtesy Doc Evans)*

Twin Terrace Cafe, October 19, 1947. From the left: Jack Goss, Earl Murphy, Bill Page, Edmond Hall, Lee, and Ed Schaeffer (Art Hodes not shown). *(Courtesy Mary Collins)*

The Kid Ory band off to Carnegie Hall, April, 1948. From the left: Little Brother Montgomery, John Schenck, Joe Darensbourg, Ed Garland, Kid Ory, Lee, Mary, Minor Hall, and Bud Scott. *(Courtesy Mary Collins)*

Frank "Sweets" Williams and Lee in Chicago, 1949. *(Courtesy Danny Barker)*

At the Club Silhouette in Chicago, May 16, 1949. From the left: Brad Gowans at the piano; *kneeling:* John Schenck, Doc Evans, Tony Parenti, Wild Bill Davison, Chet Roble, Johnny Lane, Lee, Freddie Flynn; *standing:* Brownie McGhee, Danny Alvin, Miff Mole, Doc Cenardo, Jimmy James, Bill Pfeifer, Bill Tinkler, Mama Yancey, Herb Ward (behind microphone), Bud Jacobson, Art Hodes, and Jimmy Yancey.

At the Bee Hive, Chicago, 1949. From the left: Don Ewell, Darnell Howard, Lee, Miff Mole, and Booker T. Washington. *(Courtesy Mary Collins)*

Natty Dominique and Lee. *(Courtesy Mary Collins)*

Art Hodes, Pee Wee Russell, Lee, and Georg Brunis at the Blue Note, Chicago, 1950. *(Courtesy LOOK Collection, Library of Congress. Copyright © 1950 by Cowles Communications, Inc.)*

Louis Armstrong with **Mary** and **Lee** at the Blue Note, July, 1950. *(Courtesy Mary Collins)*

Lee at the Victory Club with Sweets Williams(?), piano, and Freddie Flynn, drums, about 1951. *(Photograph by Clark Dean)*

At the Grand Theatre, Oshkosh, Wisconsin, June 18, 1951. From the left: George Winn, Lee, Dick Ruedebusch, Bob Anderson, and Art Hodes (not shown: Booker T. Washington, drums, and Jimmy Granato, clarinet). *(Photograph by John W. Miner)*

Lee at the Grand Theatre. *(Photograph by John W. Miner)*

Lee with Bill Thompson, piano, Jeep Robinson, sax, and Mama Yancey at the Jimmy Yancey Memorial Concert, Gaffer's Club, Chicago, October 6, 1951. *(Photograph by Ralph Jungheim)*

Lee with Dizzy Gillespie at the Jimmy Yancey Memorial Concert. *(Photograph by Ralph Jungheim)*

Werlie Catanese, proprietor of the Victory Club, with Lee at Lee's fiftieth birthday party, October 16, 1951. *(Photograph by Ralph Jungheim)*

5

Europe, 1951

In the fall of 1951 I got a letter from Mezz Mezzrow asking me to join his band in Paris. He said we would go on a tour of Europe and North Africa and that Zutty Singleton would be with us. This was a happy moment — I felt good to know that my old friend Zutty would be along on the tour.

Mary and I started getting ready for the trip, but my luck was still running on the wrong side. One night after leaving the Victory Club I got in Slim Collins's car along with his wife and son, a friend of theirs, and Anderson Saucier, my drummer. Slim Collins (no relation) and his wife liked to hear us play, and they would frequently wait at the club for me to get off work so that they could take me home. At 33rd and Wabash Avenue, just about halfway to my house, a car that was speeding on a cross street struck us broadside and tipped our car over. I was knocked unconscious and was taken to a hospital.

Mary was standing by my bed when I woke up; she told me that my trumpet was stolen while they were getting me to the hospital. They never did catch the guy that hit us, but, luckily, the police found my horn in a pawnshop at 37th and State Street. Mary went to the pawnbroker to get the trumpet, but first he wanted her to pay him the ten dollars he had loaned on it. She told him that was his loss because he should have had proof of ownership before taking it in. The police sided with Mary, telling the man to give her my trumpet and forget about the whole thing, which he finally did.

Zutty and his wife, Marge Creath Singleton, came through Chicago on their way to New York to catch the ship for Europe. Marge's brother, Charlie Creath, was living in Chicago at that time, so I went out to his house to see Zutty. Although we both lived in the same city, I had not seen Charlie in a long time. He told me he was sick with heart trouble.

The first time I ever met Charlie Creath, he was playing on the riverboat with Fate Marable. He was a terrific trumpet player and used to come to the Entertainers in New Orleans when I was working there. He would sit in and play with my band. He was a hell of a gambler and was known for his big cars and swell clothes.

That night at his home in Chicago, Charlie was saying how glad he was that Zutty was going to take Marge along on this trip to Europe. Little did Marge know then that it was the last time she would ever see her brother. She and Zutty were in mid-ocean when Marge received a radiogram that Charlie was dead. Marge later got a letter from her sister-in-law saying that he had killed himself. So that was a sad voyage for Marge.

Werlie, my boss from the Victory Club, came out to our house the day we left and took us to the train. Jeep Robinson, my saxophone player, was also there to see us off. I wish I could have taken him along with me; Jeep is a good musician. The last thing Werlie said to me before the train pulled out was, "Papa Lee, if you need any money while you're away, don't fail to write and let me know, because you know you can get anything from me that you need."

When we got to New York, Mary called Danny Barker and his wife, Lou, to tell them that we were in town and were sailing for France. So Danny and Lou and Omer Simeon came to see us at the hotel. I was always glad to visit with Danny because, as I have said, I was the first one to take him in a band and away from home.

We sailed the next day — and God forbid me to ever set foot on another ship! My grandfather, my father, my brother, and a cousin all sailed on ships and were good sailors, but I must confess now that no saltwater ever got into my veins. The other passengers all seemed to enjoy themselves, but I couldn't keep food on my stomach at all and was forever going to see the ship's doctor. But Mary took to the voyage like an old sailor. She liked all her meals and walked around on deck, as rough as the ocean was.

This was in October, 1951, and that old Atlantic sure did cut up some; Captain Kurt Carlsen lost his ship, the *Flying Enterprise,* that winter. If you went into the dining room to eat, you ended up on the floor. I soon forgot what my feet were made for, I was off them so much. One day, Mary got me to go to the theater, but the sea was so rough that we had to sit on the floor all during the show.

When we got near France we received a telephone call from Mezz, Zutty, and Marge (Zutty and Marge had taken an earlier boat). I could hardly hear them, but it was a good feeling to know I would soon be with my friends. It seemed like I couldn't get there fast enough so that I could stand on solid ground again. We docked in Le Havre and took the train to Paris where Mezz and the others were waiting for us.

While we were on board the ship, Mary and I met a young girl from Haiti. She was a doctor and was on her way to Liberia to a hospital there — she said that she felt she was needed there as well as in her own country. This young lady didn't speak but a little English, and I didn't speak any French. What little Creole I knew did not help. The Haitian girl and I made good traveling companions — we both could not take that rough sea. She was as sick as I was. That was the one time that Mary didn't worry about me spending some time with someone else. I think Mary really got a kick out of it, because sometimes I would catch her watching us with a half-smile on her face as if to say, "You both are too sick to get serious." And how true this was!

We told Mezz that we wanted him to help this girl after we arrived in Paris, as she had to take a train. We told him it was her first trip to France, and she could not speak any English but she could speak French. But Mezz said that French was better there anyway and she would be able to go anyplace she wanted to. I felt that Mezz had a joke on me somehow, but I couldn't find it. The last we saw of the lady doctor, she was putting her luggage in a cab, and we all waved good-bye. I can't remember her name now, but she was a nice person. Mary and I both liked her.

There was plenty to talk about that night after we got to our hotel. Zutty and I took his dog, Bringdown, out for a walk, and I thought to myself, at last, here I am in Paris, the place I always wanted to go to. Zutty and I said we were going to take Europe by storm, that we would give our best at all times.

We had a rehearsal the next day, and then we went to a small place outside of Paris to play a concert. That was the first money I made in France. I had so much money, in fact, that the bills wouldn't fit in my wallet, so the only thing to do was give it all to Mary and let her handle it. Anyway, I wanted no part of bills that didn't have the faces of dead presidents of the good old U.S.A. on them. But Marge and Mary studied the money angle of each country we toured.

On the night of that first concert I received a telegram from Hugues Panassié and Madeleine Gautier, the French jazz critics, welcoming us to France.

The next night Mary and I walked down the Boulevard Montmartre. I made a bet with her that we wouldn't see anyone that we knew from the States. But just as we reached the Rue Saint-Honoré, someone called to me, "Hey, Lee Collins." I turned around, and there was Tommy Brookins, the fine dancer that had toured with me years before with Dave Peyton's orchestra. I hadn't seen him in a long time — not after he and Ethel Waters broke up. Tommy introduced Mary and me to his dancing partner, who, I think, was from Italy. He said they were on a tour of Europe.

We also met another good friend of mine in Paris — the late Big Bill Broonzy. I knew Big Bill since the early 1930's. I never worked with him, but we did play on the same bill at the Salle Pleyel in Paris.[1] Now, Big Bill was a different style blues singer and guitar player than, say, Lonnie Johnson. Big Bill was a country blues singer; he was born where he had to suffer for the color of his face. He had hard times, he had the blues, and that is where he told the world of his troubles. One of his songs told the story of why he sang the blues:

---

[1] Lee may have forgotten that he had also been on the same bill with Broonzy at the second Bunk Johnson concert in Chicago; see p. 86.

If you are white, you're all right.
If you are brown, stick aroun'.
But if you are black, git back, git back.

One evening Big Bill and I went to the Vieux Colombier, where Sidney Bechet was rehearsing his band. After rehearsal was over I borrowed the trumpet player's trumpet and Big Bill borrowed the guitar player's guitar. I told Big Bill to play me some good old down-home blues, so he was playing and singing and I was backing him up with the trumpet. Bechet unpacked his clarinet and played along with us — he inspired me very much.

After that, Bechet took Big Bill and me to a restaurant that he always went to when he was in that part of Paris. A funny thing — Big Bill and me both got sick, so we decided we'd better go back to our hotel on the Boulevard Montmartre. I had paid the taxi fare over to the Vieux Colombier, and Big Bill said he would pay it on the way back. Now, he didn't know much about French francs, and I was no better, so when we got back in the hotel Big Bill found out that he had given the cab driver the equivalent of about ten dollars. I told him there was nothing like those good old "dead presidents," and he laughed and agreed with that. One thing about Big Bill, he was good natured and always took everything with a smile.

Besides not knowing anything about French money, Big Bill and I had one more thing in common — the only thing we ordered in the food line was ham sandwiches (*jambon,* in French). We both ate so many *jambon* sandwiches that we thought we'd never be able to look a pig in the face again!

I never expected Big Bill to pass away and leave me behind. A few weeks before he died in August, 1958, he told me that he intended to come to see me but was not feeling well himself. I was told that he had started to smoke and drink again after an operation that he had, and I knew he wouldn't live long unless he took care of himself. God has been good to me; He has kept me here on earth so far, while many of my dear friends — some that I sure thought I would beat in — are gone.

Hugues and Madeleine came up from their home at Montauban to Paris for our concert. That was my first time to meet them.

Max Jones and his wife came, too; he's a writer for *Melody Maker* magazine, London. There must have been three thousand fans in the Salle Pleyel for the Paris concert — they were sitting in the aisles and even on each other's laps, some of them. In fact, Henry Kahn, the Paris correspondent for *Melody Maker,* reported that "almost as many people were turned away from the Mezzrow-Collins-Singleton concert . . . as were admitted." Kahn also wrote: "It was immediately obvious that this combination of Mezz, Zutty, Lee Collins, André Persiany (piano), Guy Lafitte (tenor) and 'Mowgli' Jospin (trombone) was going to be good. They had played together for five days only, but there was a 'feel' and evenness in their playing. The ensemble was highly musical, it swung well and the intonation left nothing to be desired. I feel quite sure that by the end of their tour, which will take them round Switzerland, France, probably Italy, and North Africa, they will be just about as great a band as Europe can produce."[2]

We tried to slip out of the back of the hall after the concert was over, but those French fans were onto us. We got mobbed outside and Mary, being so small, was knocked down. A man named Marcel and his wife took us to a cafe the rest of the band had already managed to get to. I have to say that was our night! I will say this, too — members of the Hot Club of France and jazz clubs everywhere in Europe are loyal fans and take jazz very seriously.

The next morning we started out on our tour. We were all happy and just like one big family. Each place that we played was a big success and we received favorable writeups in all the countries we visited. Johnny Simmen, the Swiss critic for *Melody Maker,* wrote an article about our six concerts in Switzerland between November 22 and 27. He said that the concerts "were nothing short of sensational . . . Lee Collins was the greatest surprise, since not even his fine playing in 'Astoria Strut' led us to expect one of the greatest trumpet players of all time. Lee often sounds just like Louis, then shows the next minute that he is expressing himself in a style all his own, and his attack has to be heard to be believed. When Lee starts riding, you are in for the treat of your life."

What made this band so great was that it had a drummer like

[2] *Melody Maker,* December 1, 1951, p. 2.

Zutty to back it up. This bunch of musicians were with each other all the time. It was a joy to play with them, feeling each other's work the way they did.

Mary, Marge, Zutty, and me all traveled in Mezz's car. We also had a fine little Frenchman with us by the name of Paul Anash; he was our road manager. Paul would have Mezz stop at all the interesting places, and he'd tell us what century a church was built in or when a work of art was painted. That, in itself, was a great treat, because we saw plenty of old churches and castles.

After touring France, Belgium, and Switzerland, we left for Barcelona. I enjoyed this trip, especially as we were getting into a warmer climate and the highways were beautiful. I was all right until I saw the Pyrenees Mountains, and then the thought hit me that we had to go around them. There were quite a few jokes about that! The Alps were just as bad, of course.

Marge and Mary wanted Mezz to drive very slow, so we didn't have any trouble at all until we got to the French-Spanish border, where a tire blew out on us. While the tire was being fixed I watched the border guards poking long sticks into the big trucks that were loaded with boxes of grapes. The guards were checking to see if there was any smuggling going on. They sure did a good job, too.

Once the tire was fixed, we had no trouble getting across the frontier into Spain, but when we got to Barcelona we were met by the police. Right away we wondered if we had done something wrong, but the police only wanted to tell Mezz that we were expected, and then they directed us to our hotel, the Ritz. We were all tired by then, and I wanted a hot bath and a good bed.

After I woke up, some of the Hot Club members took us out to lunch at a place across the street from the hotel. I enjoyed it very much — one dish tasted like something we made in New Orleans called jambalaya. Zutty and I tried to eat all we saw of that. I went back to the hotel after lunch and sat in the lobby awhile. Pretty soon John Boles, the movie actor, came in, and we started talking. He said that he and Paulette Goddard were making a picture in Barcelona. They were staying at the Ritz Hotel, too.

The hall was packed the night of our concert in Barcelona — in fact, we never had to worry any place in Europe about what kind of audience we would have. This crowd of Spaniards screamed and stamped their feet like everything, and they even had a couple of fights. I was told that when the Spanish people act like that it means they are enjoying themselves. During intermission John Boles came backstage to congratulate us on how the band was going over and to tell us that he enjoyed the music too.

I fell in love with Barcelona and told Mary that if I had my choice of living anywhere in Europe I would take Spain. For one thing, the weather was fine, and that helped my asthma.

On the last night we spent in Barcelona, members of the Hot Club of Spain took us to a famous restaurant that was known for its chicken specialty. Everyone else ordered something different, but I asked for the chicken — it was the only thing I could think of at the moment. After we finished, the waiter brought a large book for me to autograph. In this book were the signatures of famous people from all over the world who had eaten this chicken specialty. Each one wrote a little note praising it.

After leaving Spain, we played a concert in Montauban, Panassié's home, and received a great welcome there. Mary and Marge cooked a dinner of red beans and rice, so we introduced that famous New Orleans dish to the French. Montauban is a pretty little place. The streets have tiny inlaid stones that form a beautiful pattern. I can't recall now what century the street was built in, but all the stones were laid by hand.

We did a concert in Toulouse, the home town of our saxophone player, Guy Lafitte, and then we played in the old city of Carcassonne, which looked like something out of a storybook. We visited the old castles and walked across the drawbridge over what used to be water but was dry then. Traveling in the car was a real advantage, because we got a chance to see more places than we would have going any other way.

Paul Anash took us to a place where they prepared goose in a certain way so that it took a month before it was ready to be served. This was in a very small village where the streets were so narrow that when Mezz started up with that big car of his all the other cars had to wait until he would pull into another street. But we found the place we were looking for, and the goose dish was everything Paul said it was.

It was cold and damp in Belgium when we got there, and I began to have trouble with my asthma. We had a concert to play in Louvain, but I had a severe attack, so Yannick Bruynoghe, the Belgian jazz authority, took me to see his brother, Dr. Guy Bruynoghe, of the Louvain Institute of Bacteriology. He examined me and gave me some medicine that helped me a lot. I was able to play the concert that night and make the rest of the tour okay.

In Limoges we met a kind and lovely couple — Jean and Paulette Massey — that were great fans of jazz and members of the Hot Club. We were told a wonderful story about how they lived through the Nazi occupation during World War II. The husband hid his wife in a cave, as she was Jewish, and it was heartwarming to hear how he took chances taking her food and knowing what would happen to them if they were caught.

The men in the band had been getting along together fine all this time, but then I began to notice a slight difference in Zutty. For the life of me, I could not understand why, as we had never had any words. All I wanted was to get along and blow my horn and make a good job of it. After all, that was what I went over to Europe for in the first place.

The first time I knew Zutty was angry with me was when his wife Marge saw a poster with my name billed over his. Zutty gave Mezz hell about this. Personally, I didn't care who was billed first because I was Lee Collins, the trumpet player, and he was Zutty Singleton, the drummer, and I was just as good in my field as he was in his. I got my trumpet playing from my grandfather on down, and even with asthma I was not to miss notes, as I knew all kinds of tricks with my horn. But it is not easy trying to catch your breath when you have asthma, let alone play a trumpet.

After that, Zutty and me spoke sometimes, and sometimes we did not. I wasn't drinking, so after a concert I would go straight to my hotel. The band had planned to cook a big Thanksgiving dinner at one of the French boys' homes after we got to Paris, but because of the turn that things had taken between Zutty and me, Mary and I decided to have a turkey dinner, American style, at Tom's place — a Paris supper club that was owned by an American. After leaving Tom's, we went to where Sidney Bechet was playing at the

Vieux Colombier with Claude Luter's French band. We enjoyed ourselves that night.

But after that I began to hate it that I had come to Europe. I was used to working happy, and now it seemed like every time we got to a new place something was bound to go wrong. Mezz should have known that if the musicians were happy the band would be better.

We had another concert scheduled at the Salle Pleyel, but my health was getting worse. On top of the asthma I had a cold from traveling in the car to other jobs we had. We recorded on stage during the Salle Pleyel concert, and to this day I don't know how I ever got through that night, sick as I was. The numbers we recorded were "Really the Blues," "Royal Garden Blues," "Sweet Georgia Brown" and some others.

The night of the concert I had a burning fever, and afterwards, after the job, my temperature was very high. When I got back to the hotel Mary called a doctor and he told her to either keep me in bed or get me to a hospital.

After Mary talked to the doctor she went downstairs and told Mezz and Panassié to come up to our room and see for themselves just how sick I really was. In a little while the room was full of people — there was Zutty and Marge, Big Bill, and another blues singer, Blind John Davis. I was only partly conscious by this time; sometimes I knew them, sometimes not.

Mezz asked Mary what she was going to do, and she said she was going to take me back home to the States. Everyone thought that she ought to get me to a hospital in Paris. But they didn't know Mary as well as I do — when she decides to do something, why, that is that.

I heard Marge and Zutty talking to her, wanting us to change our minds and stay because we had been so successful on our tours. But I knew that I was really sick and wasn't going to be able to travel any more for some time. Mezz told Mary that we couldn't get a ship back home so soon, but I began to think she had been looking forward to leaving before then, because she told Mezz that there was a ship leaving right away and that if we hurried we could get the boat train for Le Havre.

Marge and Zutty stayed with us after everyone else left the

room. Zutty had tears in his eyes — he really hated to see me leave. I didn't want to go, either, and wished that I was well again. Zutty told Marge to give me a hundred dollars, which she did. And I felt that Zutty and me were as good friends again as we ever were.

At noon that same day Mary and I caught the boat train for Le Havre to sail on the *Ile de France*. I was put to bed as soon as we got on the ship. The doctor told Mary the next day that it would be better for me to be downstairs in the ship's hospital, so they took me down there. I was so sick by then that I thought every minute was my last. This was the first time I saw a doctor put suction cups to my back. Mary tried to stay down there in the hospital with me, but the ocean was too rough. She got a little seasick even though she had been a good sailor on the way over.

I will have to say that everyone on the ship was wonderful to us, they did everything possible to make me comfortable. I had a male nurse that kidded me a lot and called me the "Martiniquan" because he said I looked like I came from Martinique. I kidded him right back and talked to him in my French and Creole. He got a big kick out of that. Everytime he gave me medicine he would say, joking of course, "I kill you yet before I get you back to New York." As many times that he had sailed across the Atlantic to New York, the nurse told me, he'd never set foot in the city — he always stayed aboard ship when it was docked there.

After we arrived in New York, he and another nurse had to take me off the ship in a wheelchair to a taxi, so that was where I had some fun with him. I told him that I was the first one to get him on the ground in New York. I told him he should stay and go to Chicago with us, but he said, "No, no, too many gangsters in Chicago." How funny it is that everyone always thinks of Chicago as a city of gangsters and not of the fine civic things we have there!

After we were finished with the customs, a lady offered Mary to take me to her home until she could make arrangements to get us to Chicago. Mary thanked her but said that she had cabled Trans-World Airlines for reservations. The reservations were not confirmed, though, so Mary got reservations on the New York Central Railroad instead. She took me straight to St. Luke's Hospital as soon as we arrived in Chicago. The doctor examined me and said I had double pneumonia, so I was in the hospital for some time. This was the second time that I had pneumonia.

Werlie, the boss from the Victory Club, came to see me. He was sorry that I was sick and couldn't finish out the European tour. Werlie told me that as soon as I was well again he wanted me to come back to work at the Victory Club. I stayed home trying to get my strength back for some time after getting out of St. Luke's.

I finally went back to work, but I had a kind of restlessness — which is something that had never happened to me before. I don't know exactly what it was, just a feeling that I wanted to be on the go, to do something bigger and better.

I took to going over to a cocktail lounge and barbecue place that was owned by a friend of mine named Sylvester Washington. He was one of the toughest policemen on the Chicago police force. Dan Burley, of the *Chicago Defender,* nicknamed Sylvester "Two-Gun Pete" because he was known all over the country and really kept the crooks on the run out on the South Side. Most all of the professional people went there, and I spent some nice mornings in this place, jamming with the boys in my band. That was the only place that I cared to go after getting off work in the mornings.

Early in 1952 I went to St. Louis for a little while to play in a band that Don Ewell, the pianist, had at the Barrel Club. I replaced Jack Ivett in this band. Besides Don and me there was Sid Dawson, a fine trombone player from St. Louis, Frank Chace on clarinet, and Booker T. Washington on drums. I wasn't with this band very long, and I think Dewey Jackson came in after me. I went back to the Victory Club.

About this time I had a chance to return to Europe. I got a letter from Martin Burger in Zurich, Switzerland. He wanted me to make a European tour for him with my band. We even signed contracts, and my musicians got their passports. But at that particular time Burger had Jimmy Archey and Pops Foster out on another tour and was losing money on that band, so each week I was getting more letters from him asking me to wait a little longer for my tour. I finally decided to forget the whole thing.

I was still at the same old place — the Victory Club — when Bob Maltz wrote to me, asking me to come to New York to do a concert at Town Hall in April, 1953. We had an all-star band including Georg Brunis and Jim Robinson, trombones; Albert Nicholas and George Lewis, clarinets; Joe Sullivan and Frank Signorelli, pianos; Wellman Braud and Pops Foster, basses; Zutty Singleton and George Wettling, drums; Danny Barker, banjo; and myself on trumpet. Al "Jazzbo" Collins, the famous jazz disc jockey, wrote the program notes.

After that concert I tried to talk myself into staying in New York, but I knew I would have to wait out my union card transfer. I didn't care to hang around idle that long, so Mary and I went back to Chicago.

George Lewis and his band was about to close at the Hangover Club out in San Francisco, and Doc Dougherty, the owner, was making up a band around Joe Sullivan. They needed a trumpet player, so George told Doc about me. Dougherty wrote me about going to California and wanted to know how much I would ask to play with this band. I had Mary to write back to him and give a price, including our transportation. It was okay, so I signed a contract for ten weeks. I had never played in California up to then, although Jelly Roll Morton wanted me to go out there in 1918. But I was so young at the time that I was afraid to go that far away from New Orleans. I have often regretted since then, though, that I didn't go with Morton.

The Hangover band — this was in the summer of 1953, I think — was a swinging outfit. We had Burt Johnson, trombone; Pud Brown, saxophone and clarinet; Smokey Stover, drums; Dale Jones, bass; and Sullivan, the leader, piano. Ralph Sutton, a pianist, was an added attraction.

After I was there awhile I made up my mind to remain in San Francisco. I had a friend of mine, Edgar Saucier, living there, and he asked me to stay on and make up a band with him after I closed at the Hangover. Edgar was a good alto saxophone player and had been with my band in Calumet City, so I promised him faithfully that Mary and I would stay. He invited us to move in with him at his home until we could find a place of our own. One reason I wanted to stay in San Francisco was that every Sunday we would drive out to Santa Rosa. I would lay out in the sun — a few weeks of that and I was feeling fine and like my old self again.

In the meantime, Sidney Bechet had come out to San Francisco for an engagement. I think he enjoyed himself there, too. He lived down the street from us on Bush, and we would go on lots of sightseeing trips. Sidney always had his camera with him, so he and I took a lot of pictures. We spent a good deal of time down at Fisherman's Wharf.

When we closed at the Hangover, Mary decided she wanted to go to New Orleans to visit my people. I wished to please her, so I called Edgar to tell him we were going to leave after all. He was very much disappointed and surprised because he knew I had sworn never to go back to New Orleans.

On our last night at the Hangover, Sidney and Kid Ory came over to see me — Ory was opening there right after us. That was the first time in many a year I was with two musicians that I admired so much. There was Ram Hall, too, and Ed Garland, so it seemed like old times in New Orleans again.

I hadn't had anything to drink since I had been in San Francisco, but that night all of us got drunk. Mary did not join us, saying she had to get her sleep so she could get up early in the morning. But the next morning we would have missed our train anyway if it hadn't been for a girl upstairs who woke us up. The way I felt, I wouldn't have cared if we had missed it. As it was, we made it to the station just in time. It was a good thing we had a compartment; I went to bed as soon as we got on the train.

The trip to New Orleans was very tiresome. I was so glad when I heard the conductor yell "New Orleans" — and sad after I got off the train and took one look. I was ready to get right back on a train going anywhere away from there! Everything seemed so different from when I was there last. Another bad thing too, right off, was that my brother Buddy didn't meet us at the station like we expected him to.

I had no idea where my Uncle Ernest was living and I also didn't know if the hotels were still like they used to be. If so, I didn't want to go to any one of them, but we had no other choice. So we got a cab and told the driver to take us to a first-class hotel. He drove us to a hotel on Iberville Street that looked nice from the

With Mezz Mezzrow's group in Paris, 1951. From the left: Guy Lafitte, André Persiany, Mowgli Jospin, Hugues Panassié, Lee, Zutty Singleton, and Mezz Mezzrow. *(Photograph by Jacques Wolfsohn; courtesy Len Kunstadt)*

Mary and Lee in Paris, 1951. *(Courtesy Mary Collins)*

Sidney Bechet, Dale Jones, and Lee in San Francisco, summer, 1953. *(Courtesy Mary Collins)*

At the Hangover Club, San Francisco, September, 1953. From the left: Bob McCracken, Smokey Stover, Burt Johnson, Lee, and Dale Jones. *(Courtesy Mary Collins)*

Lee with his father and his brother John in New Orleans, 1953. *(Courtesy Mary Collins)*

Brothers Theodore, Lee, and John Collins in New Orleans, 1953. *(Courtesy Mary Collins)*

At the home of Joe Mares in New Orleans, late 1953. From the left, *standing:* Joe Mares, Ricard Alexis, Jeff Riddick, Jack Delaney, Lee; *kneeling:* Harry Shields, Abbie Brunies. *(Photograph by John E. Kuhlman; courtesy Joe Mares)*

Lee at Joe Mares' home. *(Photograph by John E. Kuhlman; courtesy Joe Mares)*

front. We were assigned to a very pleasant room on the third floor, but walking up the stairs was not to my liking.

Mary and I decided to walk around and see if we could find some of our old friends, so we went down on Rampart Street and found some old-timers. They told us that quite a few musicians were working over on Bourbon Street. I hailed a cab and told the driver to take us there. He asked me to repeat that, which I did, and then he said that colored did not go cabareting on Bourbon. But he took us there anyway.

The first place we stopped at was the Paddock Lounge, 309 Bourbon, where Oscar Celestin had the band. Sonny, as we always called him, sure was glad to see me. We went in the back room where the musicians sat during intermission, and they all told me how well I was looking.

From the Paddock, Mary and me went on to the Mardi Gras Lounge, at 333 Bourbon, a few doors down the street. The band there was Willie Humphrey on clarinet, Freddie Kohlman on drums, and Thomas Jefferson, a fine little trumpet player. And my man Joe Robichaux was playing piano for Lizzie Miles, the great blues singer.

Now, it happened to be my birthday, so I will never forget that night. I had my horn with me, and the boys asked me to sit in with them. Sid Devilla, the owner, joined us with his clarinet; we really swung out some. I went back to the dressing room after we quit playing and found that Lizzie had sent out for a birthday cake for me. That was a real surprise. Everyone sang "Happy Birthday" to me, and even the patrons were sending drinks to us.

After the Mardi Gras closed that morning, Freddie and Lizzie took us to one of the exclusive restaurants where you got real Creole cooking; the cuisine there could not be beat. We saw Lizzie home, then Freddie took me to a saloon that was run by a Downtown fellow, an old-timer. His name, or rather his nickname, was Gray Eye — I mentioned him early in my story as a gang member when I was a kid in New Orleans. Of course, we could hardly get away from his place, we had so many memories of the old days to talk about.

I met Ricard Alexis, another musician friend of mine. He had used to be a cornet player, but due to an accident which injured his mouth he had to quit blowing and was playing bass fiddle. Ricard took us to our hotel but told me that he had a room to rent and that we could stay at his home. So Mary and I got our luggage at the hotel and moved to Ricard's.

By now I had been in New Orleans two days and had not seen Uncle Ernest, so I decided I better go and really hunt for him. The last place I knew about where he lived was Uptown — a place called Silver City on Derbigny Street. Across the street from Ricard's was a young musician named Howard Mendolph. He offered to take us up to Silver City to look for my uncle, but all we found there was a lot of the houses being torn down to make way for a new building project. We stopped some people that looked like old-timers to ask if anyone knew my uncle, but no one did. Finally I questioned an old-timer who did plastering work, judging by the look of his shoes. As luck had it, not only did this man know Uncle Ernest, but he had built his home for him down by the Industrial Canal and was going to see him that very evening. The Industrial Canal is quite a distance from Derbigny Street, where my uncle had lived before.

Uncle Ernest was so overjoyed to see me that he cried and wanted me to stay with him, but I told him that I still hadn't visited my father and brother across the lake. So I bought Uncle Ernest a gallon of vino — that was what he always drank — and told him we'd be back.

The next morning I got Howard Mendolph to take me across the lake to see my father and brother at Gulfport. It was a nice drive, and on the way my mind went back to the days when I had traveled the same route. It was different then, though. This is one of the most beautiful sights you could hope to see — the lake on one side and the Gulf of Mexico on the other. The highway runs along the gulf all the way to Biloxi.

Far back among beautiful shade pines and cedars are big, white antebellum homes that seem to speak of all the grandeur and splendor of days long gone by. I pictured my father and Mr. Lorenzo Tio, Sr., playing in the ballroom of one of those stately old homes, and I could almost see the fine ladies and gentlemen dancing the quadrille. I nearly wished I had been born a little earlier, but that would not have helped me any, because the barrelhouse type of

New Orleans horn I played would never have done for those elegant quadrille dances.

Riding along on the way to Gulfport, I felt like I wanted to get out of the car and wade in the gulf, so as to feel the salt water swish around my legs, and inhale the clean, fresh air. All along the bay there were people fishing or crabbing. They reminded me of an aunt on my father's side that had a lot children. Her husband used to go out and catch a big tub of crabs, shrimps, and oysters for their gumbo of a Sunday morning.

When we got to my father's place he was *so* surprised to see me. After my brother got home he explained that he had not thought I really meant to come back to New Orleans at all, so he had gone fishing instead of meeting Mary and me at the station. I spent a few hours with my father and brother and then returned to New Orleans with Howard Mendolph.

New Orleans had changed, and so had the musicians; now they were fighting among themselves all the time for jobs at the different spots on Bourbon Street. And there was nothing but jazz places and striptease joints from one end of the street to the other — it looked just like North Clark in Chicago.

I had a long talk with Ricard Alexis. He wanted me to stay on in New Orleans and make up a band, but I didn't think too much of the idea — I had now visited my relatives and, after all, that was the only reason I had come back to New Orleans. But I let Ricard talk me into the band proposition, provided that I could choose the musicians I wanted.

Ricard had been working at the Paddock Lounge, so we went to see the owners, Mr. and Mrs. Steve Valenti. But Mrs. Valenti wanted to pick the musicians — right then, I was sure that New Orleans had changed. Mary and Mrs. Valenti finally came to terms and agreed on a contract, except that we still hadn't been able to decide on a piano player. The Valentis wanted their own intermission pianist from the Paddock, and I wanted Howard Mendolph because I had heard him play and knew that he could arrange music. Mary insisted on Howard, and finally the Valentis agreed.

Then I went to Biloxi to get Alfred Williams to join the band on drums. He used to work in the old days with Sam Morgan,

Buddy Petit, Lorenzo Tio, and many other good bands that were noted in New Orleans. The rest of my band was Ricard Alexis, bass; Theodore Purnell, clarinet and saxophone; Mendolph, piano; and a trombonist whose name I can't remember.

This was a pretty good band. We had rehearsals every day at Howard's home. The boys made me think of the years gone by; we always had plenty of sandwiches and beer at rehearsals. One thing I intended to do when I came back to New Orleans was to get my fill of the oyster loafs I always loved. Howard Mendolph made this wish come true — he would bring sacks of oysters home with him, and his wife made all the oyster loafs we could eat.

As soon as we had enough rehearsals, the band opened at the Paddock Lounge, with Oscar Celestin's group taking over for us on Sundays. Now, it was my lucky break to get Sundays off, because that meant I could go and sit in that day with trumpeter Tony Almerico's band at the Parisian Room, 116 Royal Street, between Iberville and Canal. Tony had a wonderful band, along with Lizzie Miles singing as she always did — which was great. People came from all over for those Sunday sessions at the Parisian Room. Also, the band's broadcasts were heard by American boys in service overseas.

Some of the musicians who would come to play at the Parisian Room were the late George Girard, a trumpet player that had his own band at the Famous Door on Bourbon Street; Pete Fountain, a fine clarinetist; Jack Delaney, an excellent trombonist; and many, many others.

I made some recordings with Jack Delaney for Southland Records. The musicians in the band with Jack Delaney were Raymond Burke, clarinet; Stan Mendelson, piano; Abbie Brunies, drums; Sherwood Mangiapane, string bass; and myself on trumpet. We recorded four tunes: "Careless Love," "Bucktown Drag," "Who's Sorry Now," and "Basin Street Blues."

I had a lot of friends in New Orleans, of course, and everyone treated me wonderful. But it seems like any place you go there will always be someone that don't like you — I was no different from anyone else that way. One night when I was getting ready for work an old friend of mine came to visit me. We hadn't seen each other for quite a few years. We talked for a while, then he said, "Lee, I don't know exactly how to tell you this, but I understand that a certain musician is going to the 'voodoos' to do you up." I was so surprised to hear this that I had to sit down. Now, I have never believed in that sort of thing in my whole life. But there are a lot of people in New Orleans that do — and this includes all nationalities. (The history of voodoo goes way back to the days when the first slaves were brought to New Orleans, mostly from Santo Domingo, Martinique, and Guadeloupe. Many people would take their troubles and problems to voodoo witch doctors. If everything turned out like they wanted it to, they were walking advertisements for the witch doctors. The most celebrated voodoo queen of them all was Marie Laveau. Today, all the tourists who visit New Orleans go to St. Louis Cemetery to see her tomb.)

I couldn't figure out who it was had a grudge against me, as I had not been in New Orleans for over twenty years. So I decided it must have been somebody that was still mad at me from the old days when I was young and used to keep a big .38 pistol on me at all times. Now it was different; I had learned more sense than that. Anyway, I asked my friend who it was, and he finally said the person that had it in for me was a certain musician working on Bourbon Street. I got mad as hell. This man was going around telling all the other musicians that I came back to New Orleans to take their jobs away from them. Now, that was the worst, most deliberate lie that could ever have been told about me! The fact is I did not want to return to New Orleans at all and wouldn't have except for wishing to please my wife.

I had been riding to work with Ricard Alexis before hearing about this, but then I began to ride with Howard Mendolph instead; I knew I could trust him. Besides, he was like me — not scared of nothing. I was really disgusted with New Orleans by this time anyway. One or two musicians in my band began complaining about one thing and another — I don't know why, because they had better hours and I was paying them more money than they were getting before. As for me, the only real enjoyment I got was playing up to the Parisian Room with Tony Almerico and his guys.

I went over to the Roosevelt Hotel one time to play a concert, but the elevator boy wanted to know if I was white or colored. I told him that I was not white and couldn't pass for white even if I wanted to. Now, anyone from my color and up was considered there as white — if he was not a Negro. I could have said I was a Turk, and that would have been all right. But because I said I was not white, the elevator operator told me I would have to use the freight elevator. I knew I would never do that, so I started to leave. Then I heard someone call my name — it was George Girard. He wanted to know where I was going, and I told him what had happened. George turned to the elevator boy and said, "Don't you know who this is? This is Lee Collins, one of the great trumpet players of New Orleans." George and me had a laugh and went on up in the elevator with no more trouble.

I went in a little room to warm up for the concert, and then one of the musicians asked me to come out front to meet some people. First thing I knew, a girl that Mary and I remembered from Chicago came up and kissed me on the neck and sat on my lap. She didn't mean anything by it, she was only glad to see me again, but it was a good thing that the people there were high class and did not pay any attention to her. I was also glad that this hadn't happened in some joint. I thought to myself, how funny — I like not to have gotten to the concert at all because of the business about the elevator, and now, here some girl kisses me and sits on my lap.

One evening I came across a newspaper advertisement — anyone would have had to notice it because it was printed in big letters. This is the way it read: "Did you know? Five famous New Orleans trumpeteers all had much the same style originating with Buddy Bolden. The others were the fabulous Bunk Johnson, Louis Armstrong, Buddy Petit, and Lee Collins. Lee Collins is now leading his Dixielanders nightly at Steve Valenti's Paddock Lounge." I only mention this because the ad was so different and drew your attention as soon as you came to that page.

I went out one day to hunt for my friend Joe Lindsey, the drummer who worked with me in the old days. I finally found him in a barbershop on South Rampart Street. He looked well even though he had had a stroke, and I told him, "Joe, you look sharp like you always did." Joe smiled and said, "Gate, I don't care how I look, just so as I get my health back again." I gave him some money, and then we talked about old times. He told me about the death in 1952 of Herb Morand, a trumpet player who was the brother of Lizzie Miles, and I brought him up to date on the New Orleans fellows that were living in Chicago — such as Joe Milo, George Foley, and Eddie Plicque, the fight promoter.

One night a bunch of guys from the North Side of Chicago were at the Paddock Lounge; they came down for the races. They were surprised to see me in New Orleans, and we all sat at the bar and talked during intermissions. They told Mrs. Valenti that she wasn't going to be able to keep Lee Collins in this town very long. Someone else had already told the Valentis the same thing. And it was true. Steve and Mrs. Valenti were very nice to me, but the Paddock was not the place for me. I was not satisfied. We stayed at the Paddock for eight weeks, and then we left for Chicago.

6

Europe, 1954

When Mary and I returned to Chicago, I told her we weren't going to stay there long, either. In the first place, I was tired of Chicago. But the most important reason was on account of my two sons. They were not responsible for being here, so I wanted them to have all the advantages they could. It seemed like I might be able to do more for them somewhere else. Lord knows, I tried for a long time to make a go of my marriage to Lillian because of the children. Many times in my life I have wished my mother had lived so that I would have had someone to go to with my troubles and problems.

After we got settled, Mary and I learned that Lillian was in the hospital, so we went out to visit her. She told Mary that God must have sent us, that she had been very sick. Lee Collins, Jr., was away somewhere with a basketball team, and Lillian said she had not heard from him in a long time. He was like that — slow in writing — and that made Lillian worse, just worrying about him. We stayed there for a while and then I had to go and get my band together again. Lillian begged me to let Mary stay with her a little longer. I did feel sorry for Lillian, so I told Mary she could stay. Mary asked the doctor how Lillian was doing, and he replied that she was a very sick woman with maybe three months to live or maybe six. But he said that was not for him to say. Lillian died on February 18, 1954.

Now, I was always the type that had to be doing something, so I made the rounds of booking agents. But it was the same old story every place I went — nothing they offered me was enough money to leave Chicago for. So in my mind I said, what the hell, I might as well go on back to the Victory Club; I'd get as much money there as anyplace else. I took the same band back with me.

One night I came home with a high fever. I had a doctor to come in to see me the next morning, and he said that I had to have an operation, that there was no way I could get around it.

Mary and I were living in a hotel at this time, not intending to stay in Chicago. The idea of an operation worried me because I knew that the doctor bills and hospital bill, along with the expense of staying at the hotel, would work a hardship on Mary. But she never did complain about anything; she always took troubles like a trooper. Whatever suited me was all right with her.

I had given out the telephone number of Antoinette, my step-daughter, for important calls. One day she called to tell me that my bed at the hospital was ready. After I had that operation I suffered so much that to this day I am still sorry that Antoinette was home to receive that telephone call. I was a nervous wreck and couldn't have gone back to work even if I had wanted to.

Mary insisted that I go to the Mayo Clinic at Rochester, Minnesota, so one night she packed my bag and went with me to the train. That was the first time that I had gone anywhere without her — I felt very blue, and Mary kept saying, "I do wish it was so that I could go with you, Lee." I could see tears in her eyes as I left. I got a good seat on the train and tried to make myself contented, then I slept all the way to Rochester.

I got a private room with bath after my first examination at the clinic. All that week it was one examination after another. Mary came to see me the first weekend and said she liked my room and the report that the doctor gave her. But the first thing she did was get me a cheaper room. I hated to give up the room I had, but Mary was right, of course. What with the medical bills and all, it was quite an expense.

The Mayo Clinic doctors didn't find anything wrong with me except what other doctors had already found. They told Mary that I had emphysema (a dilated lung). I called Mary a few days later to come after me, as I did not feel good enough to travel alone. So she got off from her job and came up to take me home to Chicago.

Mary had received a lot of mail while I was at Mayo's. One of the letters was from Mezzrow, asking me to join him in Paris for another tour. He said he already had lined up Jimmy Archey and Freddie Moore from New York. Now, I did not have any feeling for going back to Europe, but the doctor told Mary I could go if I would take it easy. In the meantime, I was not working, just getting all the rest I could. I began to get tired of sitting around and wanted to go back to work.

Sometimes I would go out in the park and sit on a bench, and sometimes I would get with a bunch of New Orleans guys and chew the fat with them. One thing about New Orleans people — we seem to have more fun together than anyone else. And we are a clannish lot — regardless of any troubles we may have among ourselves, outsiders that interfere with us catch hell!

We made preparations to leave for Europe in the fall of 1954. I telephoned Werlie, the boss of the Victory Club, and told him I was leaving. He came out to the house to tell me he was planning a farewell party for us at the club. Mary worked the day of the party, breaking in a new girl to take her place while we were gone. She was willing to go to the party, but I could see that she was very tired, so I told her we wouldn't go.

Werlie came to take us to the train the next morning. He was a little disappointed that we hadn't got to the party, as everyone was looking for us. But I told him our reason, and he understood. Jeep Robinson, my friend and saxophone player, was also at the station to say good-bye to us.

We stayed overnight in New York at the Hotel Lincoln and went down to the ship the next morning. Pops Foster was there at the dock to see Jimmy Archey and Freddie Moore off. I hadn't laid eyes on Pops in a long time and was glad to see him again.

Remembering my first ocean voyage, I knew I was in for a rough time again, but I didn't expect to have company. It was the Haitian lady doctor that kept me company in being seasick the first crossing; this time it was Freddie Moore. Every time I had to go to the ship's hospital, Freddie was not far behind me. We tried

114

to have courage and go to the dining room, but it was no dice. Freddie and me were the most happy people when we finally got to Le Havre. But it was our bad luck to arrive late, so that meant we had to stay aboard until the next morning. The first person to welcome us was the head of the Hot Club of Le Havre, Miss Adèle Matyer. She presented Mary with a big bouquet of beautiful roses and helped every way she could to make us comfortable on the train to Paris.

We had a big laugh on the train. The customs officers came through and questioned all of us about our baggage, but Freddie Moore was the only one that had to open his. Freddie had one of those big bags with a lock that can be used either as a garment bag or a traveling bag. This one officer could not speak English, so he made motions for Freddie to open his bag. I think the customs man was just curious to see how the thing worked. Anyway, Freddie had an awful time opening the bag in that compartment — it could only hold six people and was crowded at that.

I was glad when we finally got to Paris. Mezz met us at the station with reporters and photographers; then he took us to the Royal Saint-George Hotel on the Rue Saint-George. After we had got settled we prepared for rehearsals, and Mezz told us we would tour France, Belgium, Germany, Switzerland, and North Africa. He said we were going to travel by bus this time. Now, I was not too crazy about the bus idea, but I didn't say anything, because France is a lovely country to travel through, no matter how you do it.

We got started on the tour late in 1954. In the band, besides Mezz, Archey, Moore, and me, was a Frenchman, Claude Bolling. He played piano. But I soon found out that this band was going to be a lot different from the one we had in 1951. The main difference was that everyone wanted to be a star instead of backing each other up the way it should have been. This caused a lag in our playing. Like one night I found myself out front blowing, and you couldn't hardly hear the others. But this didn't bother me any because I was so used to playing with all kinds of musicians, good and bad — and each of these guys was a good musician, in spite of their star complex. Even so, there was a tension somehow, and I didn't really know why.

On top of that, I began to have trouble with my chest again, so I started all over seeing doctors every place we went to. I knew I had made a big mistake in coming to Europe the second time. I didn't take any interest in outside events.

The band was invited out to an affair once when we were in Arles. After we finished eating, the waiter brought the bill to us! I didn't mind that so much, but we also got charged for a lot of things we had not eaten. There was even a charge for beer on my check — and I had not so much as ordered a bottle of water, let alone beer. So I told Mary that after that we would not go any place when I finished a concert.

After a concert we played in Bordeaux I was so sick that Mary and I had to leave the hotel and go hunting for a doctor. We finally found one — a German that spoke no English. However, his wife knew a little English, so Mary told her what she thought was wrong with me. When he got through examining me, the doctor told us, using his wife for an interpreter, that I had to go to a hospital. I was so sick I didn't much care where I went. The doctor's wife called the hospital and said that her husband was sending me over.

Poor Mary was so bewildered she did not know what to do, so she said that maybe I ought to wait until we got to Paris to enter a hospital; we didn't know anyone in Bordeaux. But I only wanted to get into a hospital bed right away and forget about everything. So we got a taxi and gave the driver the note that the doctor had written for us with the directions to the hospital.

On the way to the hospital, it seemed to me that Bordeaux must be our jinx. I remembered the time that Mary got a terrible tooth-ache when we were there before in 1951. Mezz and me had a hard time trying to find a dentist because all the doctors' offices happened to be closed that day. A friend of Mezz's that operated a grocery store helped us locate one. The dentist told Mary that he would have to pull the tooth without sticking in a needle to kill the pain because the tooth was abcessed at the root. So she let him pull the tooth just as it was. The amazing thing about this was that Mary wanted to eat right after the tooth came out.

When we got to the hospital, I found to my dismay that no one spoke a word of English. And, of course, I could not speak any French. For all you know, Mary told me, they may be going to cut your head off. But I didn't care; I was in a hospital, and that was all that counted. I was carried up to a room, and the nurse took my clothes away. Then I fell asleep. When I woke up later there was Mezz shaking me and telling me to get up, and Mary was standing behind him crying. Mezz called the nurse and ordered her to bring my clothes. Mezz told me he knew of a good doctor in Limoges that we would see when we got there.

From what Mary told me later when we got back to the hotel, she had gone in search of Mezz after leaving the hospital. She told him what had happened, then they came after me. The next morning we left to continue our tour. We were on the way back to Paris.

I was happy to get to Limoges and see Jean and Paulette Massey again — I told about meeting them during our 1951 tour. The Masseys had dinner for us. Mme Massey cooked a chicken specialty, besides having southern fried chicken that Taps Miller showed her how to cook when he was in Limoges. The only thing that I wanted to eat was this chicken specialty, which I called chicken jubilee. Everybody laughed about it. After dinner, the champagne flowed like water.

This was the first time that I had enjoyed myself since I had been on this European tour. There were other guests that night at the Massey's; one of them was Jean Massey's brother, who was a doctor. I told Dr. Massey about my condition, and he felt I should take a rest on the Riviera. He wanted me to stay a few weeks with a friend of his there, and he even wrote a letter of introduction for me, but I didn't go.

The concert at Limoges was a great success; the band really played that time, for a change. We started our tour of Switzerland the next morning. I was dreading it because of the cold weather; we had been to other places that were warmer. Unlike the 1951 tour, we didn't have too many concerts to play in Switzerland this time, but we did appear in Zurich, Lausanne, and Geneva.

The most of my worries were that Girard, our bus driver, was a fast driver and got a big kick out of going around the mountains at a terrific rate of speed. He would take a look at Mary's frightened face and then go all the faster in order to tease her. Otherwise, though, Mary and Girard got along fine and were the only ones that went to Mass on Sunday mornings wherever we happened to be.

By this time, Mary understood quite a bit of French. She got to the place where we could go out alone and order dinner or go shopping without any help of an interpreter. Even I got so I finally could order food in French.

When we got to the French-Swiss border to cross over into Switzerland, we found it was already closed for the night. Mezz wanted to get to Basel and spend the night there. While he was outside the bus arguing with the guards we heard two guys singing over on the Swiss side, and we could tell they were real drunk from the sound of their voices. As far as we could make out, only one of them wanted to cross over into France, but the guards would always turn him back and then his friend would get him on his bicycle and start away with him. But in a few minutes this one guy would be back again, still trying to get across. He almost made it once.

I wish I could have stayed around to see how it turned out, but Mezz finally talked the guards into letting us through, and we went on to Basel.

One thing about Switzerland, you can always find someone who speaks English. In Geneva we stopped at the Hotel de L'Ecu, which is on the lake. It was a beautiful sight to watch the swans from our window and to look up at the mountains and see the sun shining on the snow.

I had a fan of mine and Lizzie Miles's come to see me at the hotel. I was feeling very bad again, so he took me to a friend of his that was a chest doctor. I spent about an hour with this doctor and felt much better after I left his office. That night I was feeling in top shape; even Mezz and the other guys were talking about my blowing. All I ever needed was to feel a little bit good, and I would put my all in my horn — as I have said before, that was my life.

We had a concert to play in December, 1954, at the Salle Pleyel in Paris. It was snowing, and the weather was very bad when we got to Paris, but even so I think we were all happy to be back. The room Mary and I had at the Royal Saint-George Hotel was modern and comfortable as for heat — and that is unusual in France. But I couldn't rest and was having great difficulty in breathing. I wanted to get in good shape for a show we were going to do at the Olympia Music Hall. This was a big show; there were four other acts besides our band. So Mary and I decided to move to the Hotel Ronceray on the Boulevard Montmartre, the same hotel we stayed at when we were in Paris in 1951. One reason I liked the Ronceray better than the Saint-George was that at the Saint-George you could ride up on the elevator but had to walk down. At the Ronceray, though, you could ride up *and* down, which was much easier for me.

On our way over to the Ronceray Hotel we discussed it about me going to the American Hospital for a checkup, but we didn't know where it was. At the Rue Saint-Honoré we asked a policeman, and he tried to give us directions, but we could not quite understand. A few blocks further on we saw a young African man coming toward us. He was dressed very sharp and looked smart, so Mary said to me, I wonder if he can speak any English. (I thought maybe Mary was thinking about the time that we were in Paris in 1951 and I left the hotel to go to a post office. On my way back I went in the wrong direction and got lost. So I stopped an African man on the street, thinking that perhaps he was an American, and asked him the way to the Boulevard Montmartre. But he did not understand a word I was saying. Then suddenly I realized that I was standing right in front of our hotel. I had found my own way back somehow without even knowing it. I looked up at the window of our room and saw Mary watching me.)

So we stopped this African and, sure enough, it was our good luck that he spoke English. I asked him if he knew where the American Hospital was, and he said, yes, he did but that it was a long ways out. He said we could take the metro (subway) to the hospital, but that he would have to go with us to show us the way. Mary looked quite puzzled and told him, never mind, that first we had to go to the Ronceray Hotel, but he said he might as well come along with us, he had plenty of time. Then he said it would be better to take a cab. At the hotel I told him to wait for us downstairs, that we'd be right back.

As it happened, we found a girl at the hotel desk that we had known from 1951. We asked her about a room and said we'd like to get the same room we had before, if possible. I told her I was going to a hospital but that my wife would be staying at the hotel. The clerk said that someone else was in our old room, but only for a day, and that we could have another one until it was ready for us. So we decided to do that.

I asked Mary what she thought was wrong with this African man. Mary said he looked too smart and was too willing to spend a lot of time with us even though he didn't know us. She told me to stay upstairs, that she would go down and get rid of him.

Now, of course, we knew there were some smart people in Paris that were always ready to take Americans any way they could, but I had to smile at that, because I come from one of the most notorious cities in the United States, and that is New Orleans, where anything was likely to happen. So there was not much I wasn't onto, but I let Mary have her own way. She finally got shut of the African by telling him I was too sick to leave the hotel just then and had gone to bed.

We talked to the hotel manager, and he gave us directions and had a bellboy call a taxi. He said he was afraid for us to take the metro, that we might get lost as we would have to transfer to a bus in order to get to the hospital.

When we arrived there, I had to go through a lot of tests, and then the doctor said I would have to stay because I was in no condition to be any place else. I began to worry about Mary being all alone in Paris, but she said she could take care of herself and for me to take it easy and rest all I could because I had a big show to do. But I knew she was just trying to make me feel good.

I got assigned to a room with an American seaman. He was glad to have me with him because he had no one to talk to. The third man in the room wasn't able to speak English. It is funny how people from the same country are always glad to see each other, regardless of race. The reason I say that is because this man happened to be from the deep South.

Mary came to see me the next day. She had walked part of the way from the Ronceray Hotel, having forgotten which bus she was supposed to take to the hospital. Mary told me she had called Sidney Bechet, and he said to let him know if she needed anything and that he would come to visit me. Albert Nicholas was out on a tour, but I knew those Creoles would not let me down. As for the guys in Mezz's band, I didn't expect them to do anything.

I met a New Orleans fellow in the hospital. He was off a boat and was soon to be released, but not until after Christmas. I told him I expected to be out before that, but I was wrong; Mary and me had dinner together at the hospital on Christmas Day. The hospital prepared dinner for all the patients and their families so they could be together on that day. There was turkey with all the trimmings and little gifts. That was okay, but I wished I was out and blowing my horn again. I thought every day would be Christmas for me once I was well again.

Paris is especially beautiful during the holidays, what with the decorations and all. And the people have the same Christmas spirit that we do in the States. One of the most beautiful sights, which we had only to look out our window at the Ronceray Hotel every night and see, is the Sacré-Coeur Church.

At last came the big day for me to leave the hospital. I had one of the nurses call Mary and ask her to come after me, as my doctor did not want me to go back to the hotel alone. I couldn't understand why — I felt fine.

I wanted to ride the metro, never having been on it before, but the doctor said no, to take a taxi, so we did. Mary got angry with the taxi driver because he took a different direction than the one she was used to in going to and from the hotel. It turned out that the way she had been taking was longer than it should have been, but she called the driver everything she could think of. He never let on that he understood, so I told Mary I didn't care which way he went; I only had three hundred francs and that was the most he could get. Then the driver spoke up in English and said that he was taking the shortest way to the hotel. Mary and I almost fell out. I told him I was sorry for all the things my wife had said. He replied that he didn't mind, that lots of times American passengers called him all kinds of special names, thinking he did not understand them. The driver said he learned English while he was with the Americans during World War II. My little wife, who was so wise, kept very quiet all the rest of the way to the hotel!

This was the last day of December, and we knew that everyone would be out celebrating New Year's just like we did at home. I told Mary to buy herself some cognac to celebrate with, because we couldn't go out that night. I wished, though, that I could have taken her out somewhere; she had been so faithful in looking after me and didn't have time to go anyplace.

But we did have a visitor on New Year's Eve — the New Orleans seaman who had been at the hospital came to see me. Mary went out and bought some eggs and cream to make eggnog for us. She had to make three trips to get the nutmeg, as she couldn't pronounce it right in French. She finally got some by looking through sacks at the market. Then she bought some wine cakes, something I had not had since I left New Orleans. At midnight we three drank a toast to each other. Mary had her cognac, and the seaman and I had eggnog — neither of us were allowed to drink any cognac. I promised my new friend that I would look him up in New Orleans if he was there when I got back to the States. He also had a home in Havana, Cuba.

Mezz, Jimmy Archey, and Freddie Moore came to see me the next night. I wondered why — maybe it was only to find out if I was going to be able to play the Olympia Music Hall date. Freddie was the only one of the three that had come out to visit me the whole time I was in the hospital. Mezz told me that the dress rehearsal would be at Versailles, and I said I'd be ready. The date was well advertised; you could read about it on posters all over Paris. This was a big show, and I wanted to do my best — not that I didn't always, of course, but I was not as strong as I had been. This was a must for me!

Lionel Hampton and his band happened to be touring Europe at the time, and they came to Paris. One of Hampton's trumpet players, Wallace Davenport, was from New Orleans. He had heard a lot about me and wanted to meet me, so Freddie Moore brought him over to the hotel. I had heard that he was a good trumpet player, and we had a nice talk. I was always glad to see someone from home, especially a musician, so I told Davenport to hold up for New Orleans, as he knew the reputation of New Orleans trumpet players.

It had been snowing the day of the rehearsal at Versailles, and the theater was very cold, but everything went down like clockwork, and the show was good. I always did like the Nicholas Brothers' act — they were good little dancers. We went back to Paris that night, all set to open at the Olympia Music Hall with a matinee and evening show the next day. I got up early the morning of the opening, feeling real good, and cleaned my trumpet and had a good lunch. That evening at the theater everyone was in good spirits, though some of the guys did seem a little nervous. But that was something that never happened to me in all the years since I had been blowing professional.

Then we were on stage, and the band was playing Mezz's theme song, "Really the Blues," as the curtain rose. I think we had played only two numbers, and then the next one I found I could hardly get my notes out. When we came off the stage, Mezz asked how I felt, and I told him that I felt very bad and was going back to the hotel to lay down but would return in time for the next show. Mary started to pick up my horn, but I told her to leave it where it was, that we'd be coming back.

I was sure that I couldn't make it to the hotel walking, so we got a taxi. The hotel manager and his wife could tell right away that there was something real wrong with me. They said that across the street from the hotel there was a good asthma doctor — that he was very good for people that suffered with asthma — so we went over there.

As soon as we entered the place I noticed that it had kind of a weird look — like something you might see in the movies. This was one place I did not like, as sick as I was. First off, the nurse wanted to know who had sent us there, and we told her, and then she ordered me to sit down until I was called. When the doctor saw me, the first thing he did was to take a needle and draw blood from my arm and then inject it in my buttock. Now, I'd had too much dealings with real doctors not to recognize a quack when I met one, so I told Mary that we ought to get out of there. The doctor wanted me to lie down on a table and rest, but Mary said she was taking me back to the hotel, so he wrote out a prescription for me to have filled and a diet to follow.

I was getting weaker still by the time we got across the street and back to the hotel. Mary became really alarmed then and called my doctor at the American Hospital. After she explained what had happened, he said for her to rush me to the hospital as fast as she could get me there. With the help of the manager, I got in a taxi.

We told my doctor what that quack had done to me, and he was shocked. I was put to bed right away, and I don't remember anything after that.

Mary came to the hospital the next day and told me she had stayed there about an hour the night before and that then the doctor had told her to go to the hotel to get some rest. Instead, she had gone to the Olympia Music Hall to let Mezz know I would not be there for the next performance. He wasn't there, though, so Mary called his wife, Johnnymae, but she didn't know where he was, either. So then Mary telephoned Sidney Bechet, and he said he would try to find a trumpet player to fill in for me.

When Mary finally did find Mezz, he said he knew something was wrong with me when he heard me miss a note, but he didn't think it was as serious as it really was. Also, I was known to never leave my trumpet anyplace; I always took it with me wherever I went. Mezz tried to get Peanuts Holland, an American trumpet player who imitated Louis Armstrong, to take my place, but the deal didn't go through, so he finally got a French boy to fill in for me.

Mary came to see me every day at the hospital and said she was getting along okay but that she thought she would have to go to the American embassy and ask the people there to force Mezz to pay her for the week's salary I had coming. He had told her he wasn't going to pay, and I knew that Mezz was nobody's friend when it comes to money. He wouldn't pay if he could get out of it. Mezz's trouble was that he didn't know Mary, not if he was going to try to beat her out of any money. They had clashed before when we were in Europe in 1951. And Mary told me that Mezz had got away with a matter about the exchange of some Belgian francs.

I knew it would be lonesome for Mary in Paris unless she went to the movies to pass the time. There was a theater called the Californian in front of the hotel. They changed pictures there once a week; most of them were westerns. I used to kid her about those westerns. Mary told me that Mezz's wife had her over for dinner and that Peanuts Holland, Taps Miller, Lil Armstrong, and some French girl were there. I was glad she had someone to talk with instead of just sitting in her hotel room.

When I woke up the next morning — Sunday — Mary and

Sidney Bechet were there, standing by my bed. Sidney said to let him know if there was anything he could do for me. He told me he was taking Mary to his home for breakfast and to see his baby son. When Mary came to visit me the next evening she said she had been to the Vogue Record Company to collect some royalties that were due me since 1951. They had been given to Mezz, but Vogue paid her anyway. Then Mary had gone to the American embassy to tell them about the money Mezz owed us for our last trip before coming back to Paris. A man in the consul's office telephoned Mezz while she was there, asking him what his intentions were in regard to paying me the money. Mezz told him to tell Mary to come to the hotel and that he would pay her, so she went to Mezz's hotel. Mezz wanted to know why she had gone to the embassy. Mary said she was sorry she had been forced to do that, but she had warned him what would happen if he didn't pay. It would have saved them both a lot of trouble if Mezz had paid up in the first place like he should have.

I got transferred to a room that was occupied by the brother of a famous Hollywood movie director. Besides suffering from a heart ailment, this guy was also a heavy drinker, so the doctors had given him orders to drink only one jigger of cognac a day, no more. But that didn't mean anything to him, he was still pouring down a fifth a day. One morning he collapsed, and I had to ring for the nurse. The doctors found out that he not only had the fifth of cognac daily but was also smoking a pack of cigarettes a day.

I was very glad when the doctor told me, after talking it over with Mary, that he thought it would be best for me to go back to the States. Mary said that evening we would fly home. She explained that the doctor had advised her not to take me home by ship. It seemed like I was sick enough already without getting seasick to boot.

Freddie Moore was surprised when I told him that we had decided to go home. He wanted to know when I was going back to the hotel, but I said I wouldn't go there until the day we left Paris. I would only be in the way, and Mary had enough to do getting ready without having to look after me.

We had airplane reservations for January 18, so Mary came

to take me from the hospital the day before that. About an hour or so after I got back to the hotel, Mezz called and I told him we were leaving for home. Mezz promised he would come to see us before we left. For some reason, Mary seemed very nervous. She wanted to know if I felt all right and said that the manager's wife and the girl at the desk kept asking if we really had to fly home instead of returning by ship. Then Mary showed me a medal blessed by the pope that the manager's wife gave her. She got it in Rome when she and her husband were there once. Now, Mary had been in airplanes before, but not for very far, and I knew she was afraid to cross the Atlantic by air. She went out to the tobacconist's three times, but it didn't seem like she would need that many cigarettes on the trip home because in about eighteen hours we'd be in New York.

I had not made up my mind yet as to where we would go after getting back to the States. It wouldn't be Chicago, though — I never wanted to see Chicago again.

Not Mezz nor any of the other fellows in the band came to see us before we left by bus for Orly field. But all the hotel people had such a sad look on their faces when we left the Ronceray that they made me feel like I was going to my own funeral. It was raining like everything, and Paris was expecting to be flooded any minute — in fact, a lot of places already were. They told us at Orly field how lucky we were to be getting a plane out that night, because the field would be flooded the next day.

While Mary and I were in the dining room at Orly field, one of the copilots came up to us and asked if I was Lee Collins, the trumpet player. He said he would be on our plane and that he had the records I made with Jelly Roll Morton and also the Jones-Collins Astoria Hot Eight recording of "Astoria Strut." I told him I had had to cancel my tour, but he already knew about that. Everyone seemed to know about my condition, because after we were on the plane about an hour the stewardess came to me and wanted to know how I felt. She told me to let her know at once if I felt my breath getting short.

I wondered why the copilot and the other airplane people kept running back and forth along the aisle. Then, too, I heard a lot of noises that didn't sound right. Then it was announced that we were eighteen thousand feet up over the Atlantic Ocean. I remember that there were two drunks that kept running up and down the aisle; nobody could seem to keep them quiet. All of a sudden, a window popped out next to a woman that had a large dog in the seat next to her. As serious as the situation was, it looked real funny to see this woman jump over the heads of the couple in front of her. I said to myself, "Fish, here we come." But they stuffed some pillows and blankets into the hole where the window had been, and then everything was all right. Also, we heard no more out of the drunks after that — they were quieter than anyone else on the plane.

We took a cab into New York City after arriving at Idlewild. Mary insisted that we go to Chicago, but I didn't want to. Then she told me that she had shipped our trunk to New Orleans, thinking it would be better for me to go to my father's to rest up, as the weather was not as bad there as it was in Chicago. So we decided to go to New Orleans. We tried to get a plane but couldn't. Next, we attempted to get reservations on the train to Chicago and change there so Mary could see her daughter, but the only train we could get was one that would take us a long way around. So we ended up buying train tickets for Gulfport.

My brother Teddy came on the train to see me at Mobile; he just happened to be working at the station that night. I was so glad when we finally arrived in Gulfport; my feet were swollen and I was very tired. I went to bed right away and Buddy — that is, my brother John — got a doctor for me. It seemed that every doctor wanted to treat me for asthma, but that wasn't my ailment. Dr. Lipschitz, at the American Hospital in Paris, and Dr. Johnson, from St. Luke's Hospital in Chicago, were the only ones who treated me for emphysema — that was my real trouble.

I told Buddy the day after we got to Gulfport that I had decided to go to New Orleans and enter a hospital there. When we arrived on the train in New Orleans, Mary and I went to my Uncle Ernest's home. I was happy to be there with him. He looked at me with tears in his eyes; then he said, "Son, Uncle Ernest will look after you." He was married again and had a wonderful wife; she made us welcome to their home.

Uncle Ernest sold me on the idea of going to Charity Hospital, which was new and modern in every way. The doctor had told Uncle Ernest that I should be hospitalized and said he would enter me. I kind of liked it there at the hospital at first, not dreaming of the storm that was going to break over me.

The next morning a doctor came to see me. We talked for a while after he finished examining me. He said he was from Zurich, Switzerland, and that he liked jazz very much. Whenever he got the chance he would go to hear Tony Almerico's band at the Parisian Room. He asked for one of my photos, so I had Mary to bring him one.

Then the storm broke! A different doctor came in and said he was the house physician. He said he understood that I was a musician and had just come back from Europe, so I told him yes, that was true. He gave me a funny look and left.

Then a nurse came and told me I had to go downstairs to be put under a breathing machine. I knew about those machines — you had to be watched very carefully every minute you were under one of them. The nurse put me under the machine and made herself comfortable with a magazine. Then something went wrong. I couldn't call her; the only thing I could do was try to make signals to her, and it seemed to me that she would never look up from her reading. Blood gushed from my mouth after she finally took me out. Right then and there I swore I would never be put under a breathing machine again!

After this house doctor took over my case, he had the nurse to give me a different pill and shots every day, but I didn't get any better. So one day I threw away some of the pills I was supposed to take. When the doctor came, a little boy in the bed next to mine told him what I had done. The doctor stood over me with his fist drawn back and said that what I needed was my big head knocked off. He also said that if I had been a cotton picker I wouldn't be in the trouble I was. He never gave it a thought that every man is born with a heritage. I was born to be just what I was — a trumpet player. Music was handed down to me.

I told Mary and Uncle Ernest that evening what had happened. When the nurse came to give me another shot, Mary told her not to, saying she was going to take me out of that hospital. Another nurse took Mary aside and told her she thought, too, it would be best for me to leave. So the next morning my family told the doctor to write out a release, but he started in telling them all about how I had thrown away the pills, not mentioning what he had said to me. They got me ready, and then we left. I thought every step was going to be my last.

I went from Charity Hospital to Flint-Goodridge Hospital on Louisiana Avenue, one of the best hospitals for Negroes in the entire South. It was near time then for Mardi Gras, and Jack Webb was in town making a jazz movie called *Pete Kelly's Blues.* Matty Matlock, the fine white clarinet player that had been with Bob Crosby's orchestra, was looking for a band to play a funeral march in the Webb picture. Louis Armstrong told him to get Alfred Williams's band, that they were old-timers and would really play the funeral march as it should be played. Matty went to the right person; Louis would know the best men to get for that job.

One evening I heard someone calling my name — it was Alfred Williams, Ricard Alexis, and Maurice Durand. Maurice had come from San Francisco for Mardi Gras. I was happy to see them, of course, but I felt bad that I was not up to running with that bunch at Mardi Gras. I knew they would have a lot of fun.

We talked about the good old days and someone brought up the Sunday evening back in 1918 when Buddy Petit, Frankie Duson, Alfred Williams, John and Simon Marrero, and Alphonse Picou ran up against Kid Ory, Armstrong, Joe Lindsey, Bob Lyons, Lorenzo Staulz, and a Creole clarinet player named Prevo. There was a cutting contest, and everyone decided that Petit had given Ory's band a great whipping.

I had a wonderful physician at Flint-Goodridge Hospital, a Dr. Thomas. I heard about how fine the Ochsner Foundation was, and I was told that if I didn't get well there I would not get well any place. Dr. Thomas agreed with me about the Ochsner Foundation, so I went there to see about being admitted. The doctor there told me they would have me come in as soon as they could get a room ready. This was in March of 1955. I recall that our trunk had just arrived from Paris; it took from January 18 to March 20 to get to New Orleans by boat. It would have cost too much to ship it by airplane.

Louis Armstrong and Alfred Williams came to see me. Louis

said that he and Lucille had visited Joe Oliver's widow, Stella Oliver, and that he enjoyed those good old red beans and rice she cooked for them. Louis was leaving town that night. He said he was going to send me some money as soon as he got where he was going. He pressed something into my hand as he left — I looked and found it was fifty dollars. In a day or so he wired me one hundred dollars.

I decided to go back to Chicago to wait until I was notified about my room at the Ochsner Foundation. So Alfred Williams and Mary made reservations for us on the Panama Limited. Uncle Ernest and his wife came down to the station to see us off. He sure hated to see me leave, though.

After Mary and I got to Chicago and got settled, I was in hopes that maybe I wouldn't have to see another doctor — I had had enough of doctors and hospitals! Frank and June Allen and Sid Dawson came to see me often. Sid was in Chicago at that time and was working, as I remember, with Danny Alvin's band. Sid is a wonderful trombonist and someday will go down in jazz history as one of the greats.

Frank Allen wanted to give a benefit for me because my money was all gone by then. Mary was trying to work. She had gone back to her old job that she left when we went away. So Frank got an okay from Frank Holzfeind, owner of the Blue Note, to have the benefit there. Mr. Holzfeind told Frank that the money from all the liquor sold during the benefit, outside of the taxes, would go in the benefit fund for me. Joe Glaser gave the okay for Louis Armstrong to bring his band; also, all the jazz musicians in Chicago were going to play. Harry W. Gray, the president of Local 208, American Federation of Musicians, had given his consent to go ahead. The benefit was scheduled for June 6, 1955, but it fell through at the last minute, and up to this day no one seems to know exactly why. There were all sorts of rumors, though. I was told that on the night of the affair a large crowd was waiting outside the Blue Note, not knowing that the benefit was cancelled. I got hundreds of letters from fans all over for weeks after, and Mr. Holzfeind sent me many more letters that were mailed to the Blue Note for me. Joe Glaser sent one hundred dollars.

With all the money that I received in the letters, I went back to New Orleans and entered the Ochsner Foundation. I met a lot of fine people there, some from Georgia, Alabama, and other places in the South. The patients didn't take time to worry about the color of someone else's skin, and the doctors, nurses, and all of the rest of the people working there were wonderful to me. Every sick person there did their best to cooperate in every way so as to get well and be able to leave as soon as possible. After I was there a week, my doctor told me that my illness was chronic, so I felt like there was no use for me to stay any longer and keep running up hospital bills. I sent Mary a telegram that I was coming back to Chicago. Viola Jackson, a friend of Mary's, made a reservation for me on the Panama Limited, and Viola and her husband took me to the station.

Mary was waiting for me when I got to Chicago and could hardly wait for me to tell her what the doctors had said. Of course, she was hoping that it would be good news. But I didn't want to talk about it then, and Mary saw how I felt and kept silent all the way home in the cab. I was sorry for her; she had done the best she could and had worked so hard and did not spend any money on herself. All of our money went to pay for doctor and hospital bills.

Mary had prepared a nice dinner for us, but I sat there at the table hardly eating a thing. I looked over at Mary and saw tears in her eyes. I had a kind and lovely wife who was in my corner at all times, but there I was, broken in health, and nothing could be done about it. It seemed as if life was not worth living any more.

Late that same evening I got a call from Sid Dawson; he said he was glad to know I was back home. He was telling me that everyone was waiting for me to get well and play again. That hurt, because I knew I wouldn't ever play again. But for his sake I told him it would not be long before I would be back with them. I said, "Sid, tell the boys that Papa Lee is resting and rarin' to get 'Old Betsy' back in my hands again."

I was home about a week, and then I began to get restless again. I would walk around the house, but that was as far as I could go. I was still very weak. One day I called up Pete Stern, a good friend of mine, and of course he wanted to know how I was getting along. I could only tell him I was just the same. Pete asked me if I wanted to see another doctor, that he had a doctor that he would like for me to see. I told him that was all right with me, I would see this doctor, so Pete made an appointment for me. After my examination at the doctor's office he recommended that I go into a hospital. I was sure enough sick then — another hospital!

I entered Michael Reese Hospital. After I was there a few days, they gave me the same treatment that I had at the Ochsner Foundation. A week later the doctor told my wife that I had pneumonia. The one thing I wish for everyone to understand is that at no time did any of the doctors I consulted examine me for the things that I told them about. They all paid more attention to my chest condition, but I knew that nothing could be done about that.

I was ready to go home again after being cured of the pneumonia, but the doctor called my wife aside and said he would suggest that I see a psychiatrist. Now, his only reason for this was that I kept on trying to tell him where my real trouble was, but he insisted I was wrong. I tried to tell him about what had happened to me once in New Orleans when my throat got burned from a medicine that I used to spray it with. I couldn't get that through to any of the doctors, though — they seemed to think I had hallucinations. I was also very upset about Pete Stern spending all that money on me, and I could not tell him I had improved any.

I began to get more depressed every day. I felt like I had let Mary down in every respect and had become a burden to her. She was working very hard to maintain a home for us and meet the needs and necessities of life. Mary was very cheerful through it all, trying to encourage me and tell me I was going to get well and blow again. As she would say, everything is possible with God.

Mary had faith, but I was just the opposite; I went away from my teaching. I had begun to get tired of praying, and it seemed to me like God had forgotten me. Sometimes I would tell Mary, "Look, I have not committed any crimes and I have treated my fellow man all right, far as I know. But just look at all the people that do anything they want to and still have their health."

I made up my mind not to burden Mary or anyone else any more, so one morning I prepared myself to leave this world and all my troubles in it. But God is still all-powerful. Mary did not hurry up and leave as she would usually do; she seemed to wait around a little longer than usual, so I asked her why she didn't hurry and go where she was going. She gave me a funny look and asked if anything was wrong with me. I told her no, it was just that she was generally in a hurry and that it was a beautiful day out. I was afraid I had said the wrong thing and then she wouldn't go any place at all. But she finally did leave. Then I got a box of Nembutal that I had brought back from Europe. I sat down on the bed and said a prayer, then I swallowed five of the pills and lay down.

Next, the thought came to me that I should write a note to Mary and explain to her the reason why I chose the easy way out. I didn't want anyone to blame her for my death. So I went to the landlady, thinking that I ought to tell her what I had done. But I was beginning to get drowsy by that time, and my mind was so much on destroying myself that maybe I forgot what I was going to say to her. Anyway, I went back to my room and took five more Nembutals. I lay down on the bed again and went to sleep. But God did not intend for me to die, not then.

I was told later that my friend Frank Allen called for me on the telephone, and my landlady came to my room but couldn't rouse me. So she told Frank she couldn't wake me up, that I was in a stupor. Frank said for her to call a doctor and an inhalator squad and then call him back, but instead of doing that she called Mary. Then the landlady and her husband tried to revive me. Mary hurried home as quick as she could and called an ambulance. While waiting for it to arrive, she tried to stand me up and kept slapping my face.

I woke up the next morning to find myself in the psychopathic ward of Michael Reese Hospital. I was very weak and could not do much talking. The next thing I knew, I was put into a paddy wagon and transferred to the psychopathic ward of Cook County Hospital. Mary asked who it was that ordered me there, and they told her that the doctor who had treated me at Michael Reese Hospital said they should give me psychiatric treatments. I was so sick that I didn't mind staying in the hospital, any hospital, and they said I could go home as soon as I got better.

But that was not to be. In a few days, I was told that I would be sent to court. Mary, Frank Allen, and my son, Lee, Jr., came to the hospital the day for me to go to court. They said they would be there to take me home. I waited and waited but was never called into court.

Mary came back about two o'clock that afternoon and told me that the doctor had recommended that I take treatments. I wanted to know what kind of treatments, but Mary told me that they were not asked anything, that the only thing the judge had asked them was where they wanted me to go for my treatments. Not knowing what else to do, Mary had said Illinois State Hospital, because that was in Chicago.

Sending me there was about the cruelest thing that could ever have been done to a human being, because there was nothing wrong with my mind; I was as sane and sharp in the mind as I ever had been. I was still weak, though, and should have been put to bed after I was taken to Illinois State Hospital. Instead, I was handed a mop and ordered to get busy mopping the floor. I told the nurse that I had been in another hospital with pneumonia and had not long come out before getting sent there, but two big, husky guys who were there as habitual drunks and who had been made assistants grabbed me and threw me down. Then one of them kicked me in the stomach. I was too weak to be able to do anything about it, so the other assistant warned his partner not to do too much to me, that he might kill me.

One day the nurse sent me to the sick ward — that was the only place where a patient could get decent treatment. Even there, though, the assistants were cruel. There was one that didn't like policemen. There happened to be a policeman who was in bed, unable to walk. This bum, the assistant, used to beat the cop, and the poor man could not even raise a hand to defend himself.

I had a real sadist for a doctor — his main object was to keep me there. Every time I would ask him when he was going to release me, he would say, "In a few weeks." Then he would turn around and tell me that my wife was the one that put me there. If I had had something wrong with my mind I probably would have killed my wife, just because of him saying that. But I knew better than to believe him. The doctor hated Mary because she told him he was keeping me there illegally. She went to the superintendent and asked him to have a talk with me in order to prove that I was okay, but he never called me in for the talk.

I was given permission to walk around the grounds because it was summer and very hot. One thing I found out was that there were people who had been at the hospital so long that they were completely forgotten about. I met one young man that had been there twenty years. He was allowed to leave the grounds daytimes, though, to sell newspapers. I don't know why he was never released. I never asked him, either; I soon learned that it was best not to ask questions or talk too much if you wanted to get along there. Anyway, this man used to bring my dinners to me from the outside. I didn't eat the food they served at the hospital — it wasn't fit to eat.

I was very much depressed, and one day when Mary came to visit me I told her I couldn't stand it there any longer. I could see she was feeling the same way I did. She asked if I would be afraid to walk away because it seemed like we were not getting any place in trying to arrange with the doctors for my release. The only thing was that the Sunday before this some men that were real tough had escaped from the hospital and the police were looking for them, as they had guns and one of them was out to kill his wife. It was lucky that the police finally caught them.

Mary and me didn't know if we would be stopped or not. We decided to try it anyway, so we walked across the hospital grounds, and the first person we met was the young man that brought me my dinner every day. I told him I was on my way to the ward and would see him when I got back. He asked if Mary would want dinner too, as she ate with me sometimes when she came to visit. But Mary told him she wouldn't have time, and I said not to order for me, either, because I was feeling too bad to eat. I didn't want him to spend his money, as the dinner would have been on him, and that seemed like a dirty trick to play on the only friend I had there.

Mary was trembling; she was that frightened when we got to the gate. I spoke to the guards and wished them good day, then we walked across the street to catch a bus. I just stood there a minute and took a deep breath to inhale free air again. It was good to be among free people that were sane.

Mary decided we could not go home; we were afraid they would be looking for me because I didn't have a release from the hospital. So we went to my aunt's home. She was surprised and glad to see me. After a good, hot bath and something to eat, I went to bed. Believe me, it was a grand feeling to get in bed again between clean, smooth sheets.

When Mary came back from work the next morning I asked her to call a good friend of mine downtown and to tell him what happened and that I wanted him to see what he could do for me. Then I went out to Cook County Hospital, where I was admitted to the chest ward as a very sick man.

In the meantime, this friend of mine I spoke of called Mary and said that he had got a lawyer to look after my case. The lawyer filed a suit against the hospital and the superintendent, and the matter was taken into court. During the hearing, the lawyer for the state told the court that they wanted to drop the whole thing. He told the judge that I would never be bothered again. Later on, Mary was called to the Illinois State Hospital to get the papers signed for my official release.

I received the best of care in the chest ward of Cook County Hospital. The nurses were very considerate, but I was on the downgrade and it didn't look like I would improve any.

One day, my friend Frank Chace got word to me that he and some other musicians of Local 10 were going to put on a benefit for me. They knew I was heavily in debt and had no way of paying my bills. All the money I had was already gone for medical and hospital bills, and I was still in debt. The concert was held June 30, 1957, at the Glenbard Firehouse on Roosevelt Road in Lombard, Illinois. All my good friends from Local 10 were there: Frank Chace, Georg Brunis, Danny Alvin, Jimmy Ille, Floyd O'Brien, Jimmy Granato, the Dukes of Dixieland, the Salty Dogs, and many others. From my own Local 208 was Franz Jackson, Al Wynn, Sweets Williams, and Baby Dodds.

During the height of the concert, the nurses brought me to a telephone so I could listen to a number that the Dukes of Dixieland dedicated to me. After hearing a great part of the music I felt so blue; in my heart I was wishing that I could be there playing instead of someone playing for me. Instead of being happy, I was worse, so I asked the nurses to take me back to my bed. But I was grateful to all the musicians that took part in the benefit. I was told later that the concert had been a great success and that the place was packed, with many people that couldn't get seats having to stand up all around the walls.

The next day, the newspapermen and photographers came out to the hospital to see me. I was very ill, but whenever anyone wanted to talk to me about jazz, I was always ready, regardless of how I felt. That was my life and the way that I lived.

Epilogue

Lee Collins's last days were painful and frustrating. His final public appearance was the concert at Olympia Hall in Paris on December 4, 1954, at which he became ill after playing several numbers. From that time on he was in and out of various hospitals in Chicago and New Orleans. Although forbidden to blow his trumpet, Lee continued to hope that someday he would be able to play again.

On Sunday, July 3, 1960, Lee suffered a stroke and passed away at his home, 1424 East Marquette Street, Chicago. He was buried July 8 in Holy Sepulchre Cemetery, Worth, Illinois, with fellow musicians and other friends attending the funeral.

Lee Collins will be remembered as a member of the early generation of musicians who marched in funeral processions and parades, played the clubs and cafes, and contributed to the development and dissemination of the New Orleans style of jazz. He played an important part as well in the jazz life of Chicago, the city which became his "second home." It was, in fact, while Collins was working at a tavern on North Clark Street called the Victory Club that he achieved international fame. Between the years 1945 and 1954 visits from traveling musicians and foreign dignitaries were frequent, and hundreds of jazzmen — from Bunk Johnson, Louis Armstrong, Miff Mole, Dizzy Gillespie, down to the younger musicians learning their trade — came to jam with the pioneer hornman from New Orleans.

"Papa Lee" also made a great impression in Europe in his two brief concert tours there in 1951-52 and 1954. The headline in one French newspaper is representative of his reception on the Continent: "Avec Lee Collins, Bayonne a entendu un grand artiste de l'époque héroïque de la Nouvelle-Orléans."

His name will go down in jazz history alongside other early trumpet "Kings" in the lineage — Buddy Bolden, Bunk Johnson, Freddie Keppard, Buddy Petit, Louis Armstrong. And the sound of his horn will be perpetuated by his performances on the phonorecordings which he left behind.

Mary Collins summed up her husband's career with the words: "His life was his trumpet." Fortunately for so many, it was a life he was always willing to share.

Afterword

In the world of sport, when time stands still between events, enthusiasts are often tempted to play the Best-Ever game, jotting down great names of yesterday or today in the realms of cricket, football, motor racing, or maybe "the horses," and drawing up present-day world teams or national squads. In jazz circles, too, this listing of names that count—from all-time greats to promising newcomers—is nothing new; in fact, it is about as old as jazz literature itself. Indeed, we suffer a surfeit of polls and awards, for Musician or Record of the Year, Best Instrumentalist, Band, or Singer, and so forth. No doubt these hotchpotches of personal opinion, prejudice, hype, and statistics afford worthwhile publicity for a number of jazz artists, but they confuse rather than clarify the subject for those seeking enlightenment and pleasure.

I found myself reflecting on popularity polls, critics' awards, and the like while re-reading this revealing story of the life and hard times of Lee Collins. Not much chance for him in the polls: he made too few recordings for that and cut his best long ago. But to me he was quite an important figure in jazz history—a semi-legendary figure until I met him in France some thirty-eight years ago. Though not hidebound in his musical tastes, Papa Lee had an upbringing in a certain type of jazz and believed in that tradition. I wonder how we can seek to grade players who even have conflicting notions of what real jazz is.

For the benefit of American readers I have to stress that for years the jazz listening of elderly British fans like me was limited to gramophone records and the radio, with occasional injections of "live" music, and that many records were unknown here, many others hard to get. Samples of Collins's trumpet work were very scarce. As late as 1942 Stanley Dance (in our *Jazz Music* magazine) was asking for the release "of the much-requested Jones-Collins items." I considered myself lucky to be acquainted with these and, later on, imported copies of the 1924 Mortons (not impressive) plus one Chippie Hill and one Century disc featuring Lee. They bred in me a strong respect for a man with the authentic sound, beat, and spirit of New Orleans in his playing. This respect for a then-almost-forgotten figure steeped in the artistry of Oliver, Armstrong, and, it was said, Bunk Johnson stirred me to visit Paris during November 1951 in order to report on the Mezz Mezzrow band and interview its trumpeter. The welcome from Lee and Mary Collins exceded all expectations. And Papa Lee's playing, more powerful than I had anticipated and filled with what I took to be down-home know-how, dominated the music.

Not for the first time, the difference between hearing jazz on records and experiencing it "live" struck me forcefully. "Time for the trumpet solo came," I wrote in *The Melody Maker* that December, "and it needed only three or four bars to tell me that here was the real thing in New Orleans trumpet. The tone was hot and pretty big, with a kind of crackling vibrato on the long notes that I had noticed with Armstrong and Bechet when hearing them in person. The feeling was right too, and there was the dragged timing and off-the-beat swing of Armstrong's blues playing [also] some of the quality of the last Tommy Ladnier performances, and here and there a run in the Henry Allen tradition."

Lee himself swore allegiance to Bunk, telling me: "He was my inspiration. Louis and I grew up together, always played in that way. I guess it came from Bolden." Obviously, beginning on trumpet at about twelve years old and getting his first gigs two or three years later, Collins could not have been influenced by an Armstrong of the same age, much less by a younger Red Allen. And to me he did not readily admit the debt he came to owe to Louis. As for Allen, I'm sure Lee never expressed admiration for him and tended to change conversational tack if the name cropped up.

As Papa Lee impressed me with his fair-mindedness in general, his deep interest in jazz, and his shrewd judgement of its practitioners, I guessed he had personal reasons—probably linked to his few months' stay with Luis Russell's band in 1930—for by-passing this subject. His stint with Russell was not happy: J. C. Higginbotham and Allen (for whom Lee was deputizing at the Saratoga Club, at least for part of his time with the band) both stated separately during the sixties that Collins was "a bad reader and, for this reason, Luis Russell had to let him go." And Christopher Hillman, in the book *Bunk Johnson*, writes: "Lee Collins developed his style into one of extreme expressive excitement, but when he was asked to substitute for Allen in Russell's band he found his inability to read an insuperable hurdle; he ended his days finding what work he could in the rough Chicago clubs."

In truth, I still recognize many little similarities to Red's flourishing tone and spicy phraseology in Collins's fine lead and solo work on "Duet Stomp" and other tracks by the Jones and Collins octet; and since Lee came quite close to Louis in certain passages, I assume he was familiar with some of the Hot Five and Seven series of recordings. However, differences in Lee's attack, his ways of mixing his phrases and of producing a personal timbre, make clear that the trumpet we respond to on these charmingly old-style New Orleans performances is distinctive and sometimes oddly tender-sounding, as in "Damp Weather" and "Tip Easy."[1]

British author John Chilton, my collaborator on the book *Louis*, recently told me, "I don't think Lee copied anyone; yet, fascinatingly, because he shared the same heritage as Louis, Bunk, Ladnier, and Allen, I can always hear something of these musicians when I listen to him." Swiss writer John Simmen adds: "I hear some typical Henry Allen stuff in his playing here and there, and believe he tried to get away from being cast as a pure Louis follower. Louis was Lee's god but he must have realised there was no chance of measuring up to his idol; so he would lean on Red. . . . In our talks Lee would express various opinions, but when he stated, 'Louis has always been ahead of us all, and he still is!' I could tell this was his true conviction."

In trying to place in perspective this view of a musician I think of as holding an honoured place in the roll call of second-generation Crescent City jazzmen, I have no wish to undermine his standing in

the eyes of critics and historians. Quite the contrary. Rather, I want
to underline the part chance plays in the selection of those destined
for fame and fortune. Because of a combination of bad luck and
music-reading problems, celebrity status eluded Collins. Trombonist
Preston Jackson confirmed that Lee could barely "read" and that
this held him back in the thirties and forties so far as big-band work
was concerned. This disability affected his career in other ways also.

Collins enjoyed a short concert tour he made in 1948 with Kid
Ory's band; most of the men were in high spirits (and well into spirits, too, it seems). Lee tells that the leader wished him to continue,
but he said no. "I regret to this day that I did not go with Ory,
because jazz had begun to decline in Chicago." However, the band's
clarinettist, Joe Darensbourg, gave another account in his autobiog-
raphy: "Lee Collins had a helluva time because Ory had all of these
tunes written out and Lee couldn't read nothing. . . . We settled for
tunes that he really could play, like 'Cornet Chop Suey,' and I don't
think I ever seen anybody play them much better. Lee was a real
nice guy." Almost everyone agreed about the trumpeter's amiability.
Whatever the truth might have been, Lee's failure to remain with
Ory was an example of ill luck and, perhaps, poor tactics. It allowed
the rewards reaped by so many musicians from the New Orleans
(or traditional jazz) Revival to pass him by, and since numbers of
"revivalists"—among them hometown veterans such as Papa Mutt
Carey—were indifferent readers at best, Fate would appear to have
allotted him a permanent place in the shade.

This kind of misfortune dogged him almost from his start in
the jazz big time—in Chicago, from September 1924, with King
Oliver. On that Christmas Eve the Lincoln Gardens burned down,
and Lee was soon looking for work. He made no records with
Oliver, did the session with Jelly Roll but missed the notable Peppers
dates which could have made his reputation, and, instead of perse-
vering in Chicago, returned to New Orleans early in 1925. Appar-
ently he stayed too long down in Louisiana, Texas, and Florida. Although in 1929 he recorded the four titles generally regarded as
Collins classics, by the time he tried New York and returned to
Chicago, he had failed to establish his name and times were getting
tougher.

Throughout the thirties and forties, Lee never went rusty

and seldom stopped working, though some of the jobs were back-breakingly hard. He wound up with a lengthy residency at the Victory Club on North Clark Street in Chicago. A 1948 *Down Beat* reported that the band played there seven nights a week from about 8 P.M. to 4 A.M. "There is no such thing as a 'set' at the Victory," the writer claimed, adding that a food break was the only rest. John Chilton reminds me that the late Dick Wellstood once went round to the club, excited by the prospect of hearing and talking to L. C., and to his dismay found that the working schedule was so tight that Lee had to eat his sandwiches on the bandstand.

Collins came directly from that engagement to Europe in 1951, and at once it was clear he was far from well—another example of "outrageous fortune." He was taken sick on both tours, and the emphysema impaired the musical level of the records cut in France between 1951 and 1954.[2] As was his way, Lee smiled at trouble and applied himself body and soul to the tasks at hand until forced to enter hospital.

In spite of the setbacks Lee was uplifted by his reception in Europe, on and off the stage, and delighted by the attention paid him by fans, hanging on his every word. For Lee, the music was a way of life, and I don't believe he considered any other. "Leaving aside for a moment his serious health worries, he must have had some of the finest moments of his life on these visits," says John Simmen. "He *loved* speaking about music with aficionados, and never tired of it. I promise you it was a thrilling experience to listen to Pops's records with him. Today, when I hear Collins's records—the Jones-Collins sides and four for Century are my favourites—and think back on the concerts with Mezz, I have the memory of a man devoted to his craft. A dedicated musician, he meant everything he said or played, and I recall this side of Lee with admiration and affection." For me, too, it was an experience to treasure: Lee was a terrific person, under-valued and under-rewarded in material things. I tried to find him work in Britain, but the "ban" on foreign jazzmen still operated, and it was lifted (in 1956) too late to help him—another golden opportunity denied a man who was not often in the right place at the right time.

To return to the Best-Ever game, there would be no sense in debating Lee's place in the ranks of the greats of all periods, but we can try to assess his importance among those who learned jazz in the same regions and at about the same time. The consensus I found locally is that he was a middle-order player, perhaps in a class with men like Herb Morand and Punch Miller, deserving of wider recognition. To give John Chilton the last words: "In that exalted world of Louisiana trumpeters I would place Collins in the top dozen; he was under-recorded and never received much publicity. However, he proved in the fifties that he had lasted the course well despite years of semi-obscurity playing in small Chicago clubs."

MAX JONES

Notes

1. The appearance of alternative takes of this pair of titles gives an insight into how carefully L. C. built his melodic solo contributions. With regard to the body and boldness of his tone here, I realize that the sound obtained in recordings in the dance hall might give a false impression.

2. In spite of the limitations some potent, sweeping, even fiercely blasted horn is to be heard in "Struttin' with Some Barbecue," "If I Could Be with You," some blues tracks on the 1951 Vogue album, and even occasionally on the "Victory Club" LP.

Discography

Abbreviations

INSTRUMENTS		RECORD LABELS			
as	alto saxophone	Auto.	Autograph	Riv.	Riverside
bj	banjo	Bb.	Bluebird	Ses.	Session
cl	clarinet	Bm.	Biltmore	So.	Southland
d	drums	BN	Blue Note	Sp.	Spivey
p	piano	Cen.	Century	Tem.	Tempo
sb	string bass	Cir.	Circle	Vic.	Victor
t	trumpet	Col.	Columbia	Voc.	Vocalion
tb	trombone	HMV	His Master's Voice		
ts	tenor saxophone	JC	Jazz Collector		
v	vocal	JS	Jazz Selection		

COMMERCIAL RECORDINGS
(compiled by Brian A. L. Rust)

JELLY ROLL MORTON'S KINGS OF JAZZ: Lee Collins, t; Roy Palmer,
   tb; "Balls" Ball, cl; Alex Poole, as; Jelly Roll Morton, p.
   Chicago, ca. September, 1924

635	"Fish Tail Blues"	Auto. 606; Ses. 2; JC L-25;
		Tem. R-19; Riv. 12-128; Rhapsody RHA-6021
636	"High Society"	As above
638	"Weary Blues"	Auto. 607; Ses. 4 (not issued),
		Rhapsody RHA-6021
639	"Tiger Rag"	As above

IMPERIAL SERENADERS: Probably: Lee Collins, t; George Lewis, cl; Tink Baptiste, p; Alex Scott, bj; Roy Evans, d.
New Orleans, September 23, 1925
140991-1-2 "Climax Rag"   Col. rejected

JONES AND COLLINS ASTORIA HOT EIGHT: Lee Collins, t; Sidney Arodin, cl; Theodore Purnell, as; David Jones, ts; Joe Robichaux, p; Emanuel Sayles, bj; Al Morgan, sb, v; Joe Strode-Raphael ———, d.
New Orleans, November 15, 1929
BVE-56534-1 "Astoria Strut"   Vic. V-38576; Bb. B-8168; HMV 7EG-8084, Bm. 1001; "X" LVA 3029
BVE-56535-1 "Duet Stomp" (Morgan, v)   As above, RBF 203
BVE-56536 "Damp Weather"   As above
BVE-56537- "Tip Easy Blues"   As in "Duet Stomp"; Vic. LEJ 3, Camden CAL 385

BLUE SCOTT AND HIS BLUE BOYS: Leonard Scott, v, accompanied by Lee Collins, t; unknown ts; Richard M. Jones, p.
Chicago, August 5, 1936
BS-100677-1 "I Can Dish It — Can You Take It?"   Bb. B-6520
BS-100678-1 "You Can't Lose"   Bb. B-6557

RICHARD M. JONES, v, accompanied by Lee Collins, t; unknown ts/own p.
Chicago, August 5, 1936
BS-100681-1 "Trouble in Mind"   Bb. B-6569
BS-100682-1 "Black Rider"   Bb. B-6569, B-6963

HANNAH MAY AND THE STATE STREET FOUR: Addie "Sweet Peas" Spivey, v, accompanied by (probably) Lee Collins, t; Arnett Nelson, cl; J. H. Shayne, p; John Lindsay, sb.
Chicago, August 20, 1936
C-1447-1 "Just a Rank Stud"   Voc. 03313
C-1448-1 "Kansas City Hill"   Voc. 03313

JANE LUCAS AND THE STATE STREET FOUR: According to the recording files, this is Victoria Spivey, although it does not sound very much like her, accompanied by (probably) Lee Collins, t; J. H. Shayne, p; John Lindsay, sb; unknown d.
Chicago, August 20, 1936
C-1449-1 "Dreaming of You"   Voc. 03314; Sp. LP 2001
C-1450-2 "I Can't Last Long"   Voc. 03314; Sp. LP 2001
(NOTE: The liner notes to Spivey LP 2001 give Victoria Spivey, v; Lee Collins, t; Dorothy Scott and Sweet Peas Spivey, p; Bud Washington, d; unknown sb. *Ed.*)

LIL JOHNSON, v, accompanied by Lee Collins, t; J. H. Shayne, p; probably
    John Lindsay, sb.
    Chicago, September 16, 1936

C-1467-2	"Black and Evil Blues"	Voc. 03374
C-1468-2	"You're Just a Cream Puff" ("You	Voc. 03374
	Can't Take It")	
C-1469-	"Can't Read, Can't Write"	Voc. 03331
C-1470-	"Ramblin' Man Blues"	Voc. 03331

VICTORIA SPIVEY, v, accompanied by Lee Collins, t; Arnett Nelson, cl;
    J. H. Shayne, p; John Lindsay, sb.
    Chicago, October 15, 1936

test	"Detroit Moan"	Sp. LP 2001

BERTHA "CHIPPIE" HILL, v, accompanied by Lee Collins, t; Lovie Austin
    or J. H. Shayne, p; John Lindsay, sb; Baby Dodds, d.
    Chicago, February 5, 1946

C-1-A-1	"Trouble in Mind" (Austin, p)	Cir. J-1003
C-2-A-1	"Careless Love" (Austin, p)	Cir. J-1004
C-4-A-2	"Charleston Blues" (Shayne, p)	Cir. J-1004
C-5-1	"How Long Blues" (Shayne, p)	Cir. J-1003
C-7-	"Around the Clock Blues" (Austin, p)	Cir. J-1013
C-8-	"Nobody Knows You When You're	
	Down and Out" (Austin, p)	Rejected

    (NOTE: The sides on which Lovie Austin plays are labeled as ac-
    companied by Lovie Austin's Blues Serenaders; those with J. H. Shayne,
    as accompanied by Baby Dodds's Stompers. Matrices C-3 and C-6 are
    piano solos by J. H. Shayne.)

EURREAL "LITTLE BROTHER" MONTGOMERY'S QUINTET: Lee
    Collins, t; Oliver Alcorn, cl, ts; Little Brother Montgomery, p, v; Ernest
    Crawford, sb; Jerome Smith, d.
    Chicago, March, 1947

1-DS	"El Ritmo"	Cen. 4009
2-DS	"Swingin' with Lee"	Cen. 4010
3-DS	"Long Time Ago" (Montgomery, v)	Cen. 4009
4-DS	"Woman That I Love"	Cen. 4010

MEZZ MEZZROW AND HIS BAND: Lee Collins, t; Mowgli Jospin, tb;
    Mezz Mezzrow, cl; Guy Lafitte, ts; André Persiany, p; Zutty Single-
    ton, d.
    Paris, November 15, 1951

51-V-4145	"Boogie Parisien"	Vogue V-5114, LDM-30002

51-V-4146	"Clarinet Marmalade"*	Vogue V-5114, V-2352, LDM-30002, LD-037, LD-518
51-V-4147	"If I Could Be with You"	Vogue V-5111, LDM-30002, EPL-7084; BN BLP-7023
51-V-4148	"Struttin' with Some Barbecue"	Vogue V-5112, V-2099, LD-037, LD-518, LDM-30002
51-V-4149	"The Sheik of Araby"	Vogue V-5113, V-2100, EPL-7084, EPL-7595, LD-037, LDM-30002

Paris, November 16, 1951

51-V-4150	"Blues Jam"*	Vogue V-5111, V-2100, LD-037, LDM-30002; BN BLP-7023
51-V-4151	"Revolutionary Blues No. 2"	JS 822
51-V-4152	"Blues No One Dug"	Vogue V-5112, LDM-30002; BN BLP-7023
51-V-4153	"Mezzerola Blues"	Vogue V-5113, EPL-7084, LDM-30002; BN BLP-7023
51-V-4154	"Drum Face"	Vogue V-5115, V-45-610, EPL-7595, LD-037
51-V-4155	"Blues in the Twenties" ("Blues des anées 20")	Vogue V-5115, V-2099, CBM-60007, LD-037, LDM-30002; BN BLP-7023

(NOTE: Sides marked * differ between the original 78 rpm issues and subsequent LPs; Vogue V-45-610 and EPL-7595 as by Zutty Singleton and his Orchestra.)

Salle Pleyel, Paris, February 5, 1952
Claude Bolling, p, replaces Persiany

"Really the Blues" ("Gone Away Blues")	Vogue LD-070
"Royal Garden Blues"	Vogue LD-070
"Sweet Georgia Brown"	Vogue LD-070
"Muskrat Ramble"	Vogue LD-070
"I've Found a New Baby"	Vogue LD-070

Algiers, later in 1952
André Persiany, p, replaces Bolling
     "Royal Garden Blues"/"Goin' Away Blues"
     "The Sheik"/"None of My Jelly Roll"
     "If I Had You"/"Muskrat Ramble"

(NOTE: The above six sides were coupled as shown and issued only to members of the Hot Club de France in North Africa. Only 100 copies of each were pressed.) (*ED. NOTE:* These are tunes known to be in Collins's repertoire. However, Collins never mentions being in Algiers, nor does Mary Collins remember visiting there. Also, Collins left Europe shortly after the Salle Pleyel concert, February 5, 1952.)

JACK DELANEY: Lee Collins, t; Jack Delaney, tb; Raymond Burke, cl; Stan
    Mendelson, p; Abbie Brunies, d; Sherwood Mangiapane, sb.
    New Orleans, November 15, 1953

"Who's Sorry Now"	So. 101, So. SLP 201, So. SLP 214
"Careless Love"	So. 100, So. SLP 201, So. SLP 214
"Bucktown Drag"	So. 100, So. SLP 201, So. SLP 214
"Basin Street Blues"	So. 100, So. SLP 201, So. SLP 214

PRIVATE RECORDINGS
(Compiled by Frank J. Gillis)

1948   March; Chicago; recorded by Bill Page; one wire spool (15 minutes);
Lee Collins and Mary Collins speaking.
"Nobody Knows You When You're Down and Out,"* "You'll Never
Know" — *a capella* vocals by Lee Collins. (Original in possession of Bill
Page; copy in Indiana University Archives of Traditional Music.)

1949   October 12; Bee Hive Club, Chicago; rec. by James D. Gordon; two
wire spools (1½ hours); Lee Collins, t; Miff Mole, tb; Darnell Howard,
cl; Don Ewell, p; Booker T. Washington, d.
"Dinah," "Ain't Gonna' Give Nobody None o' My Jellyroll," "Ain't
Misbehavin'," "Indiana," "Dippermouth Blues," "Cherry," "You're
Some Pretty Doll," "Fidgety Feet." (Original in possession of James
D. Gordon.)

1950   Bee Hive Club, Chicago; radio broadcast (½ hour); date, personnel,
titles unknown. (Copies in possession of Boris Rose and Roy Morser.)

1951   March (?); Chicago; rec. by Richard A. Waterman; two wire spools
(1½ hours); interview. (Originals in Indiana University Archives of
Traditional Music; copy in Tulane University Archive of New Orleans
Jazz.)

1951   July 7; Gaffer's Lounge, Chicago; rec. by Barbara Reid (approximately 1
hour); Lee Collins, t; Scotty McGlory, cl; George Winn, tb; Don Ewell,
p; Booker T. Washington, d.
"Panama," "High Society," "Ain't Gonna' Give Nobody None o' My
Jellyroll,"* "On the Sunny Side of the Street," "Struttin' with Some Barbecue," "When It's Sleepy Time Down South," "Way Down Yonder in
New Orleans," "That's a Plenty." (Originals or copies in Tulane University Archive of New Orleans Jazz.) *Note:* Titles from this session were
issued on side B of a 12-inch LP disc (New Orleans Records NOR 7203)
entitled *Lee Collins: A Night at the Victory Club.*

* Included on the soundsheet (MAL 741) with this book by permission of
the performers, the recorders, and the American Federation of Musicians.

1951 July 28; Gaffer's Lounge, Chicago; rec. by Barbara Reid (approximately 1 hour); Lee Collins, t; Jeep Robinson, ts; Bill "Nose" Thompson, p; Anderson Saucier, d; Charlie McBride, v; others (?).

"Blue Turning Grey," "Victory Club Blues," "Clark Street Blues," "Struttin' with Some Barbecue," "For You My Love," "High Society," "When I Lost My Baby," "When the Saints Go Marching In." (Originals or copies in Tulane University Archive of New Orleans Jazz.)

1951 August 1; Gaffer's Lounge, Chicago; rec. by Barbara Reid (approximately 1 hour); personnel as above.

"After You've Gone," "Clark Street Blues," "Blue Turning Grey," "Victory Club Blues," "If You Were Mine," "Blues," "Do You Know What It Means to Miss New Orleans," "Muskrat Ramble," "Way Down Yonder in New Orleans," "Be My Own," "After You've Gone." (Originals or copies in Tulane University Archive of New Orleans Jazz.)

1951 August 10; Victory Club, Chicago; rec. by Barbara Reid (approximately 1 hour); personnel as above.

"A♭ Blues," "Storyville Blues," "Red Sails in the Sunset," "For You My Love," "The World Is Waiting for the Sunrise," "Royal Garden Blues," "I Wish That I Could Shimmy Like My Sister Kate." (Originals or copies in Tulane University Archive of New Orleans Jazz.)

1951 October 6; Gaffer's Lounge, Chicago; rec. by Barbara Reid (?) (approximately 1 hour); Lee Collins–Dizzy Gillespie, t; Sid Dawson, tb; Jeep Robinson (?), ts; Bill "Nose" Thompson (?), p; Booker T. Washington, d; others (?).

"High Society," "After You've Gone," "I Found a New Baby," "Struttin' with Some Barbecue," "Blue Turning Grey," "When the Saints Go Marching In" (Mama Yancey, v). (Originals or copies in Tulane University Archives of New Orleans Jazz.)

1952 March(?); Barrel Club(?), Saint Louis; radio broadcast (½ hour); Lee Collins, t; probably Sid Dawson, tb; Frank Chace, cl; Don Ewell, p; Booker T. Washington, d.

Titles unknown. (Copies in possession of Boris Rose and Roy Morser.)

1953 August 1; Hangover Club, San Francisco; radio broadcast (½ hour); Lee Collins, t; Burt Johnson, tb; Pud Brown, cl, ts; Dale Jones, sb; Ralph Sutton, p; Smokey Stover, d.

"Panama,"* "After You've Gone," "Little Rock Getaway" (Joe Sullivan, p solo), "West End Blues," "Indiana." (Boris Rose and Roy Morser.)

1953 August 8; Hangover Club, San Francisco; radio broadcast (½ hour); personnel as above.

"Down in Jungle Town," "St. James Infirmary," "Honeysuckle Rose" (Joe Sullivan, p solo), "Johnson Rag," "Sunny Side of the Street," "Hindustan" (incomplete). (Boris Rose and Roy Morser.)

* Included on the soundsheet (MAL 741) with this book by permission of the performers, the recorders, and the American Federation of Musicians.

1953   August 15; Hangover Club, San Francisco; radio broadcast (½ hour); personnel as above.
"I Found a New Baby," "Buddy Bolden's Blues," "Muskrat Ramble," "Monday Date," "Clarinet Marmalade." (Boris Rose and Roy Morser.)

1953   August 22; Hangover Club, San Francisco; radio broadcast (½ hour); personnel as above except Bob McCracken, cl, replaces Pud Brown; Don Ewell, p, replaces Ralph Sutton.
"Fidgety Feet," "Chinatown My Chinatown," "Viper's Drag" (Ralph Sutton, p solo), "Basin Street Blues," "Big Butter and Egg Man." (Boris Rose and Roy Morser.)

1953   August 29; Hangover Club, San Francisco; radio broadcast (½ hour); personnel as above.
"Royal Garden Blues," "If I Could Be with You," "Bucket's Got a Hole In It," "After You've Gone," "Save It Pretty Mama." (Boris Rose and Roy Morser.)

1953   September 5; Hangover Club, San Francisco; radio broadcast (½ hour); personnel as above.
"Original Dixieland One-Step," "Fidgety Feet," "Dark Eyes" (Meade Lux Lewis, p solo), "St. James Infirmary," "Indiana." (Boris Rose and Roy Morser.)

1953   September 12; Hangover Club, San Francisco; radio broadcast (½ hour); personnel as above.
"Dippermouth Blues," "Ballin' the Jack," "St. Louis Blues" (Meade Lux Lewis, p solo), "Lulu White Blues," "When the Saints Go Marching In." (Boris Rose and Roy Morser.)

1953   September 19; Hangover Club, San Francisco; radio broadcast (½ hour); personnel as above.
"Sweet Georgia Brown," "Down in Jungle Town," "Squeeze Me," "Six Wheel Chaser" (Meade Lux Lewis, p solo), "I Found a New Baby" (incomplete). (Boris Rose and Roy Morser.)

1953   September 26; Hangover Club, San Francisco; radio broadcast (½ hour); personnel as above.
"Sheik of Araby," "West End Blues," "After Hours" (Meade Lux Lewis or Don Ewell, p solo), "Darktown Strutters' Ball." (Boris Rose and Roy Morser.)

1958   June 2; Chicago; rec. by Bill Russell; one tape roll (¾ hour); interview. (Copy in Tulane University Archive of New Orleans Jazz.)

Bibliography

Anonymous. "Bands Blare Out at Collins Benefit," *New Orleans Item,* July 1, 1957, p. 30.
———. "Benefit Set for Ailing Jazz Man," *New Orleans Item,* June 24, 1957, p. 3.
———. "Big Benefit Set for Lee Collins," *Down Beat,* Vol. 22, No. 12 (June 15, 1955), p. 6.
———. "Jazz Days Over for Lee Collins; Veteran Trumpeter Has Dilated Lung," *New Orleans Times-Picayune,* June 24, 1957, p. 37.
———. "Lee Collins Joins Don Ewell Group," *Down Beat,* Vol. 19, No. 7 (April 4, 1952), p. 8.
———. "Papa Lee Too," *Melody Maker,* Vol. 34 (August 22, 1959), p. 14.
———. "Wife's Book to Carry Lee Collins' Tune," *Chicago Sun-Times,* January 4, 1959.
Beall, George E. "Forgotten Giants," *Jazz Information,* Vol. 2, No. 11 (December 20, 1940), pp. 12-20. Pages 18-19 concern Lee Collins.
———. "Lee Collins," *Jazz Music,* Vol. 7, No. 1 (January–February, 1956), pp. 7-8. Reprinted from the *Bulletin du Hot Club de France.*
Collins, Lee. "Zutty Didn't Tell Truth about Europe Trip, Says Lee Collins," *Down Beat,* Vol. 20, No. 8 (April 22, 1953), pp. 1, 45. Answer to article by Louise La Salle.
Collins, Mary, and John W. Miner, eds. "From Lee Collins' Story," *Evergreen Review,* Vol. 35 (March, 1965), pp. 66-71.
"Doc." "N. Clark Jazz Will Lose Its 'King' when Lee Goes," *Down Beat,* Vol. 15, No. 25 (December 15, 1948), p. 3.
Hoefer, George. "Lee Collins Marks His 35th Year as Jazzman," *Down Beat,* Vol. 18, No. 21 (October 19, 1951), p. 13.

Jones, Max. "A Great Jazzman — and He Only Finds Fame after 50! Max Jones Begins the Story of Lee Collins," *Melody Maker,* Vol. 27 (December 8, 1951), p. 9; "Continuing the Lee Collins Story," December 22, 1951, p. 9; December 29, 1951, p. 5.

———. "The Triumph of a Veteran," *Melody Maker,* Vol. 27 (November 24, 1951), p. 3.

Kahn, Henry. "Mezz Wanted to Show He Could Play That Thing . . . ," *Melody Maker,* Vol. 27 (December 1, 1951), p. 2.

La Salle, Louise. "Zutty Singleton Returns from France Disillusioned and Bitter at Mezzrow," *Down Beat,* Vol. 20, No. 4 (February 25, 1953), pp. 1, 6. Information on Lee Collins in Europe in 1951.

Miner, John. "Ailing Trumpet Player Appeared on Program Here," *Oshkosh Daily Northwestern,* June 26, 1957, p. 4.

Panassié, Hugues. "Lee Collins, notable seguidor de Armstrong," *Ritmo y Melodia* (Barcelona), No. 57 (December, 1951), p. 3.

Obituary articles appeared in:

Bulletin du Hot Club de France (Paris), 3d ser., No. 100 (September, 1960), p. 12.

Chicago Sun-Times, July 4, 1960, p. 35.

Coda (Toronto), August, 1960, pp. 28-29.

Down Beat, Vol. 27, No. 19 (August 18, 1960), p. 15.

Jazz Magazine (Paris),Vol. 6 (September, 1960), p. 11.

Jazz Report (Ventura, California), Vol. 1, No. 7 (March, 1961), [p. 16].

Melody Maker, Vol. 35 (July 16, 1960), p. 10.

Musica Jazz (Milan), Vol. 16 (August–September, 1960), p. 16.

Second Line (New Orleans), Vol. 11, No. 11-12 (November–December, 1960), pp. 9, 23.

Variety, Vol. 219 (July 13, 1960), p. 63.

Index

Acey (bass), 29
Advertising wagons, 49-51, 55
Alcorn, Oliver (clarinet), 60, 85, 87
"Alexander's Ragtime Band," 19
Alexis, Ricard (cornet, string bass), 105-6, 108, 109, 129
Allegretti, Bon Bon, 69
Allen, Elmo (drums), 68, 77
Allen, Frank, 130, 133
Allen, Henry, Sr. (cornet), 52
Allen, Henry "Red" (cornet, trumpet), 52, 65, 73, 81
Allen, June, 130
All Star Cabaret (Chicago), 72
"All the Whores Like the Way I Jazz," 15
Almerico, Tony (trumpet), 108, 109, 128
Alvin, Danny (drums), 130, 136
American Hospital (Paris), 119-21, 123-25, 127
Ammons, Albert (piano), 67
Anash, Paul, 97, 98
Anderson, Bob (trumpet), 90
Archey, Jimmy (trombone), 102, 114, 122
Arles, France, 116
Arlington, Josie, 24
Armstrong, Lil (Mrs. Louis, first wife), 67, 71, 124
Armstrong, Louis (cornet, trumpet), 11, 17, 18, 20, 25, 28, 33, 34, 35, 36, 47, 50, 52, 54, 55, 56, 67, 68, 71, 76, 80, 96, 110, 124, 129-30, 138-39
Armstrong, Lucille (Mrs. Louis, second wife), 130

Arodin, Sidney (clarinet), 32, 48
"Around the Clock Blues," 86
Astoria Gardens (New Orleans), 47-49, 63. *See also* Jones-Collins Astoria Hot Eight
"Astoria Strut," 48, 50, 96, 126
Atkins, Eddie (trombone), 58
"At the Animals' Ball," 5
Audubon Park (New Orleans), 21
Austin, Lovie (piano), 86

Ball, Balls (clarinet), 38
"Ballin' the Jack," 11
Banner, Charlie, 69
Baptiste, Tink (piano), 26
Barbarin, Isidore (baritone horn), 59
Barbarin, Paul (drums), 44, 59, 60, 65
Barbee, William (piano), 69
Barcelona, Spain, 97-98
Barker, Danny (banjo), 42n, 44, 47-49, 92, 103
Barker, Lou (Mrs. Danny), 92
Barksdale, Everett (guitar), 71
Barnum and Bailey Circus, 49
Barrel Club (St. Louis), 102
Basel, Switzerland, 118
Basie, Count (bandleader, piano), 66
"Basin Street Blues," 108
Battle House (Mobile, Ala.), 28
Battles of music (New Orleans), 16, 49-51, 129
Bayonne, France, 139
Bechet, Sidney (clarinet, soprano sax),

Index

Books in the Series Music in American Life